COTSWOLD TRAVEL GUIDE

2024 Edition

Cotswolds Uncovered: From Honey-Colored Cottages to Rolling Hills, Uncover the History, and Hidden Gems of England's Quintessential Countryside

By

D1608148

Roy McKean

TABLE OF CONTENT

MUST VISIT DESTINATIONS

CHAPTER FOUR

NAVIGATING COTSWOLDS

CHAPTER FIVE

ACCOMMODATION

DISCLAIMER

Welcome to our immersive travel guide! As you embark on this journey through the pages of Cotswolds travel guide, we want to set clear expectations. While we aim to transport you to captivating destinations and provide valuable insights, we do so without the aid of maps and images.

Why, you ask?

Our intention is simple: to stimulate your imagination and curiosity. By omitting maps, we encourage you to rely on your instincts, engage with locals, and discover hidden gems beyond the well-trodden paths. Instead of images, we invite you to paint vivid mental pictures through words and descriptions, allowing your mind to craft its unique interpretation of the places we explore.

In this text-centric guide, we prioritize storytelling, history, culture, and practical advice. We believe that your own perceptions and interpretations will make your travels more personal and memorable. It's an invitation to be present in the moment, to interact with your surroundings, and to embrace the serendipitous adventures that come your way.

So, as you delve into these pages, let your imagination soar, and let the words be your compass in this world of exploration and discovery. Bon voyage!

INTRODUCTION

Welcome to the Cotswolds

In the heart of England lies the Cotswolds, a region of unparalleled allure. Its undulating hills, adorned with cottages of honey-hued stone, and storybook villages, form an enchanting tableau that speaks to the soul of rural England. Here, travelers are transported to a realm of timeless beauty and quintessential charm. With each step, history resonates through the cobbled streets and ancient architecture, whispering tales of a bygone era. The Cotswolds stand as a living testament to the harmonious coexistence of man and nature.

This cherished landscape, wreathed in natural splendor, invites exploration and introspection. Wildflowers sway in the breeze, painting the fields with a kaleidoscope of colors, while ancient woodlands offer sanctuary to both flora and fauna. The Cotswolds are not merely a destination; they are an experience, an immersion into a world where time seems to pause, allowing for a profound connection with the land.

Tradition and modernity successfully coexist in this place. Visitors take part in an authentic trip through the area's rich culinary legacy, whether they are savoring a hearty dinner in a centuries-old inn or perusing the booths of a bustling farmers' market. A haven for weary travelers, a place of solace for the soul, and a place where memories are woven into the very fabric of the land are the Cotswolds

Why Cotswolds?

A Tapestry of Timeless Beauty

The Cotswolds are a living tapestry of architectural and natural beauty, where every village seems to have sprung from the pages of a storybook. The enchanting honey-hued limestone buildings, each with its own story to tell, evoke a sense of stepping back in time to a world of tranquility and grace.

Idyllic Villages Steeped in History

Each village in the Cotswolds boasts its own distinctive character and history. From the fairytale-like village of Bibury, with its iconic Arlington Row, to the market town majesty of Stow-on-the-Wold, every corner invites exploration and promises a glimpse into centuries of heritage.

Unspoiled Natural Splendor

Beyond the charming villages, the Cotswolds reveal a landscape of breathtaking natural beauty. The rolling hills, carpeted with wildflowers in spring and golden fields in summer, are crisscrossed with walking trails and dotted with ancient woodlands, providing endless opportunities for exploration and moments of serenity.

Culinary Delights and Time-Honored Traditions

The Cotswolds are not only a feast for the eyes but also a treat for the taste buds. From indulging in traditional afternoon tea to savoring local produce at bustling farmers' markets, the region offers a culinary journey steeped in tradition and flavor.

Gateway to Historic Landmarks

In close proximity to the Cotswolds lie some of England's most significant historic landmarks. Blenheim Palace, birthplace of Winston Churchill, stands as a testament to Baroque grandeur, while Sudeley Castle whispers tales of royalty and romance. These architectural marvels provide a window into England's rich and storied past.

A Sanctuary of Tranquility

The Cotswolds provide respite from the hustle and bustle of modern life. Here, time slows down, and the gentle pace of the countryside allows for moments of reflection, relaxation, and a profound connection with nature.

A Warm Welcome Awaits

As you embark on your journey through the Cotswolds, you'll find a warm and welcoming community ready to share their stories, traditions, and the magic of this cherished region. Whether you're strolling through the charming streets or gazing upon the rolling hills, you'll feel the heart and soul of the Cotswolds enveloping you, leaving you with memories to cherish for a lifetime.

So, welcome to the Cotswolds, where the past meets the present in a timeless embrace, and every corner reveals a new story waiting to be discovered. Allow the magic of this region to unfold before you, and let its beauty captivate your heart.

CHAPTER ONE

PLANNING YOUR COTSWOLDS ADVENTURE

1.1 Setting Your Travel Goals

Before embarking on your Cotswolds adventure, taking the time to define your travel goals lays a solid foundation for an enriching experience. Reflect on what you hope to achieve during your journey by considering the following questions:

Are you yearning for a serene retreat amidst the tranquil countryside, where time slows, and nature's beauty takes center stage? Alternatively, does your heart beat faster at the thought of immersing yourself in the rich tapestry of history and culture that the Cotswolds offer, with its ancient architecture and storied past?

Perhaps your palate longs to savor the culinary delights that grace the region's charming eateries, from traditional pubs serving hearty fare to refined dining establishments showcasing local flavors. Or, do you envision your days filled with invigorating nature hikes, where each step unveils a new vista, and every hill promises panoramic views of this picturesque landscape?

Maybe your soul seeks solace in the embrace of a quaint village, where cobblestone streets wind their way past honey-hued cottages, and the rhythm of life moves at its own gentle pace. Or, are there specific activities and events that have piqued your interest, whether it be a local festival, an artisan workshop, or a leisurely boat ride along a meandering river?

By answering these questions and setting clear travel goals, you pave the way for a tailored itinerary that aligns precisely with your interests and aspirations. Every moment in the Cotswolds becomes a purposeful step towards realizing the experience you've envisioned, ensuring that your journey through this idyllic English countryside is nothing short of extraordinary.

1.2 Choosing the Best Time to Visit

The Cotswolds, a region of undulating hills, enchanting villages, and timeless charm, offers a captivating experience year-round. Each season paints its own unique portrait, ensuring that regardless of when you choose to visit, you'll be met with distinct beauty and a range of experiences tailored to your preferences.

Spring (March to May): A Tapestry of Renewal

As winter's grasp loosens, the Cotswolds awakens in a burst of color and vitality. The countryside transforms into a living canvas, adorned with a profusion of blooming flowers. Daffodils sway in the meadows, cherry blossoms grace the orchards, and bluebells carpet the ancient woodlands. The landscape, resplendent in shades of green, exudes a palpable sense of renewal.

The milder temperatures of spring make it an ideal time for leisurely walks and explorations. The air is crisp, yet filled with the promise of warmer days ahead. It's a season of budding life, with lambs frolicking in the fields and songbirds serenading the awakening earth. Those seeking a tranquil escape amidst nature's revival will find spring in the Cotswolds a veritable paradise.

Summer (June to August): The Peak of Abundance

As the sun graces the Cotswold sky for extended hours, summer bathes the region in golden light. Days are long, allowing for unhurried explorations and the chance to revel in the abundant offerings of the countryside. Outdoor festivals and events dot the calendar, providing an opportunity to immerse yourself in the local culture and traditions.

Villages come alive with the laughter of children, the melodies of street performers, and the aromas of blooming gardens. Gardens and parks are at their zenith, boasting a riot of colors and fragrances. It's a season for al fresco dining, where you can savor the flavors of the Cotswolds amidst the backdrop of its resplendent scenery. Whether it's a leisurely stroll along the banks of a tranquil river or a more challenging hike through the undulating hills, summer invites you to embrace the fullness of the Cotswold experience.

Autumn (September to November): Nature's Grand Finale

As the days grow shorter, the Cotswolds dons its autumnal robe, painting the landscape in rich hues of red, gold, and amber. The trees, adorned in their vibrant foliage, create a tapestry of breathtaking beauty. With fewer crowds, there's a sense of quiet introspection that permeates the countryside, allowing for a deeper connection with nature.

Autumn in the Cotswolds is a time of harvest festivals and country fairs, where the bounty of the land is celebrated. The scent of wood smoke mingles with the earthy fragrance of fallen leaves, creating an atmosphere of cozy intimacy. It's a season for long walks through the rustling woods and evenings spent by a crackling fire. Those who appreciate the interplay of nature's elements will find autumn an enchanting time to explore the Cotswolds.

Winter (December to February): A Time of Intimate Charm

As winter descends upon the Cotswolds, the region takes on a different kind of magic. Villages adorned with twinkling lights exude a warm and inviting atmosphere. The possibility of snow lends an ethereal quality to the landscape, turning it into a winter wonderland.

Cozy pubs beckon with crackling fires, offering refuge from the brisk air. The pace of life slows, allowing for moments of quiet reflection and connection with the community. Christmas markets and festivities infuse the villages with a sense of merriment and camaraderie. Winter in the Cotswolds is an opportunity to experience the region's intimate charm and the enduring spirit of its inhabitants.

When planning your Cotswolds adventure, consider the palette of experiences that each season offers. Whether it's the vibrant renewal of spring, the abundance of summer, the grand finale of autumn, or the intimate charm of winter, there's a time for every traveler to uncover the Cotswolds' hidden treasures. Allow your preferences and desired experiences to guide you in selecting the perfect season for your journey through this timeless English countryside.

1.3 Visa and Entry Requirements

Embarking on a journey to the Cotswolds requires careful preparation, and one of the paramount steps is understanding the visa and entry requirements. Ensuring compliance with these regulations is essential to a seamless and hassle-free adventure in this idyllic English countryside.

1. Visa Requirements: Navigating Entry Protocol

Before setting foot in the UK, it's crucial to ascertain whether you require a visa for entry. Visa regulations vary depending on your nationality, purpose of visit, and the duration of your stay. A visit to the official website of the UK government or consultation with the nearest British consulate or embassy can provide you with precise information tailored to your specific circumstances.

Should a visa be necessary, it's imperative to initiate the application process well in advance of your intended travel dates. This allows ample time for processing and ensures that all required documents, including passport-sized photos, financial statements, and accommodation reservations, are in order. Failing to address visa requirements in a timely manner may result in delays or, in worst-case scenarios, an inability to embark on your Cotswolds adventure as planned.

2. Passport Preparedness: Your Key to Entry

Your passport serves as the gateway to the Cotswolds, and its validity is of paramount importance. Prior to making any travel arrangements, confirm that your passport remains valid for the entire duration of your stay in the UK. Some countries require a certain period of validity beyond your intended departure date, so consulting your government's travel advisory or passport office is prudent.

Moreover, ensure that your passport contains an adequate number of blank pages to accommodate immigration stamps and visas. An insufficient number of pages may lead to complications upon entry. If your passport is nearing expiration or lacks the necessary blank pages, promptly seek renewal or apply for additional pages through your respective passport authority.

3. Safeguarding with Travel Insurance: A Prudent Precaution

While embarking on a journey to the Cotswolds promises unforgettable experiences, unforeseen circumstances can arise. To safeguard against unexpected events, consider acquiring comprehensive travel insurance. This invaluable precautionary measure offers protection in the event of trip cancellations, medical emergencies, lost or delayed luggage, and a range of other unforeseen occurrences.

When selecting a travel insurance policy, scrutinize the coverage details to ensure it aligns with your specific needs and activities planned during your stay in the Cotswolds. Verify that the policy extends to the entirety of your trip, including any additional excursions or activities you intend to undertake. Moreover, be aware of any exclusions or limitations to the coverage and consider supplementary policies if needed.

By addressing these essential considerations before booking your Cotswolds adventure, you fortify the foundation of your journey with meticulous planning and foresight. This proactive approach not only ensures compliance with visa and entry requirements but also provides peace of mind, allowing you to immerse yourself fully in the beauty and charm of this timeless English countryside. With the logistical groundwork laid, you are poised to embark on an exploration of the Cotswolds that is as seamless as it is enchanting.

1.4 Budgeting and Money Matters

Budgeting and managing your finances are crucial aspects of planning a successful Cotswolds adventure. This involves a careful assessment of various expenditures and the implementation of effective financial strategies to ensure a seamless and enjoyable trip.

1. Establishing a Realistic Budget: To begin, create a comprehensive budget that covers all aspects of your trip. This should include accommodation, transportation, dining, activities, and souvenirs. Allocate funds to each category based on your preferences and priorities. It's advisable to also include a contingency allowance for unexpected expenses or spontaneous opportunities that may arise during your journey.

2. Accommodation: The Cotswolds offers a wide range of lodging options to cater to different budgets and preferences. From charming bed-and-breakfasts and boutique inns to self-catering cottages and budget-friendly hostels, there's a variety of choices available. Carefully selecting

accommodation that aligns with your financial plan ensures a comfortable stay without straining your budget.

3. Dining: Embrace the opportunity to indulge in the local cuisine of the Cotswolds. While occasional gourmet experiences can be a highlight of your journey, balance it with meals at local pubs and cafes to manage expenses. This approach allows you to savor the richness of the culinary offerings without exceeding your budgetary limits.

4. Transportation: Plan your transportation in advance to optimize your budget. Research various options such as train passes, bus tickets, and car rentals to identify the most cost-effective and convenient mode of travel within the Cotswolds. Additionally, consider exploring the region on foot or by bicycle for a budget-friendly and immersive experience in the picturesque countryside.

5. Activities and Attractions: Engage in activities and visit attractions that align with your interests without breaking the bank. Research free or low-cost attractions, scenic walks, and cultural experiences. Additionally, consider purchasing a sightseeing pass if it offers value and convenience for the specific places you plan to visit.

6. Souvenirs and Mementos: Allocate a portion of your budget for souvenirs, gifts, and keepsakes to commemorate your Cotswolds adventure. Handcrafted items and local products make for meaningful tokens of your journey, allowing you to bring a piece of the Cotswolds home with you.

7. Contingency Fund: It's prudent to set aside a portion of your budget as a contingency fund to cover unexpected

expenses or last-minute opportunities that may enhance your experience. This ensures that you're prepared for unforeseen circumstances without straining your overall budget.

8. Currency Exchange and Payment Methods: Familiarize yourself with currency exchange rates and the availability of ATMs in the Cotswolds. Consider carrying a combination of cash and using credit or debit cards for added flexibility in managing your expenses.

9. Monitoring Expenses: Keep a vigilant eye on your expenses throughout your journey to ensure that you stay within budget. Utilize mobile apps or maintain a travel journal to record expenditures and maintain financial discipline.

By approaching budgeting with diligence and foresight, you can strike a balance between enjoying the richness of the Cotswolds experience and managing your finances effectively. This thoughtful approach ensures that your journey through this idyllic English countryside is not only memorable but also financially sustainable. With your financial groundwork laid, you're poised for an adventure that combines the best of exploration and fiscal prudence.

1.5 Essential Packing Tips

Packing for your Cotswolds adventure requires careful consideration to ensure you have everything you need for a comfortable and enjoyable trip. These essential packing tips will help you make the most of your journey through this idyllic English countryside.

1. Seasonal Wardrobe Selection: Consider the time of year you'll be visiting the Cotswolds. Pack clothing appropriate for the season, ensuring you have layers for potential temperature fluctuations. In spring, bring light layers, while summer calls for breathable fabrics. Autumn requires warmer attire, and winter demands cozy clothing, including a reliable coat.

2. Comfortable Footwear: Whether you're exploring charming villages or traversing scenic trails, comfortable and supportive footwear is crucial. Bring a pair of sturdy walking shoes or boots for countryside adventures, and don't forget comfortable everyday shoes for leisurely strolls.

3. Weather-Appropriate Gear: Be prepared for any weather conditions that may arise during your journey. If you're visiting in the cooler months, pack a waterproof and insulated jacket. In warmer weather, bring a sun hat, sunglasses, and sunscreen to protect against the sun's rays.

4. Adaptable Attire for Different Activities: Pack versatile clothing that suits various activities. Consider outfits that can transition from casual sightseeing to more formal occasions, like a nice dinner or a cultural event.

5. Practical Accessories: Bring a backpack or day bag for outings, ensuring you have essentials like a water bottle, sunscreen, a map, and any other necessities close at hand. A reusable water bottle is both eco-friendly and convenient for staying hydrated.

6. Electronic Essentials: Don't forget to pack your chargers and adapters for electronic devices such as phones, cameras,

and laptops. A power bank can be invaluable for keeping your devices charged while exploring.

7. Travel Documents and Essentials: Keep all essential travel documents organized and easily accessible. This includes your passport, visa (if required), travel insurance, accommodation reservations, and any relevant medical documents. Consider using a travel wallet or organizer to keep everything in one place.

8. Toiletries and Personal Care: Bring a compact toiletry kit with essentials like toothbrush, toothpaste, shampoo, conditioner, soap, and any specific personal care items you require. Remember to pack any necessary medications and a small first-aid kit for minor injuries or ailments.

9. Travel-Friendly Luggage Options: Choose luggage that suits your travel style. A rolling suitcase is convenient for paved streets and urban areas, while a backpack or duffle bag is more versatile for exploring off the beaten path. Consider a daypack for excursions and daily essentials.

10. Entertainment and Leisure: Bring items for entertainment during downtime, such as a book, journal, or travel guide about the Cotswolds. Consider packing a deck of cards or a small travel game for leisurely moments.

11. Personal Touches and Comforts: Include personal items that make you feel at home, like a favorite scarf or a special keepsake. These small touches can enhance your sense of comfort and well-being during your travels.

By adhering to these essential packing tips, you'll be well-prepared for your Cotswolds adventure. Remember to pack thoughtfully, keeping in mind the activities you have planned and the season in which you'll be visiting. This ensures a comfortable, enjoyable, and memorable journey through the enchanting English countryside.

CHAPTER TWO

GETTING ACQUAINTED WITH COTSWOLD

2.1 Overview of Cotswolds

Stretching across the heart of England, the Cotswolds is a geographical gem that encapsulates the very essence of rural splendor. This area of unparalleled natural beauty lies nestled in the south-central expanse of England, forming a landscape that is both captivating and idyllic. Distinguished by its undulating hills, the Cotswolds beckon visitors with a patchwork quilt of emerald fields, hedgerows, and woodlands, creating a picturesque tableau at every turn.

One of the Cotswolds' most enchanting features is the architectural marvel of its villages and towns. Built from the locally quarried honey-colored limestone, the buildings exude a warm and inviting glow, especially in the soft hues of twilight. This distinctive stone, a hallmark of the region, bestows an ageless charm upon the Cotswolds, as if time itself has chosen to linger here.

Beyond its aesthetic allure, the Cotswolds are steeped in history and cultural significance. With roots stretching back a millennium, the area flourished during the Middle Ages, primarily due to the thriving wool industry. This prosperity is evident in the grandeur of the stately homes, historic churches, and market squares that grace the region. Each structure tells a story, bearing witness to the resilience and creativity of the people who once called this place home.

Today, the Cotswolds stand as a living testament to this legacy, where history is revered and celebrated. Artisans and craftsmen continue to ply their trades, keeping alive age-old techniques in the creation of textiles, ceramics, and other traditional crafts. This cultural thread, woven through the fabric of daily life, creates a palpable sense of continuity with the past.

For travelers seeking an authentic English experience, the Cotswolds stand as an unrivaled destination. Its serene countryside, coupled with the richness of its cultural heritage, offers a unique and immersive journey into the heart of England. With each step through its charming villages and market towns, visitors are transported to a world where time seems to have slowed, inviting them to savor the beauty and history that define this remarkable region. The Cotswolds is not just a place; it's an experience, an encounter with a living tapestry of nature, culture, and architectural splendor that will leave an indelible mark on every visitor.

2.2 Historical and Cultural Background

The Cotswolds unfurls a vivid tapestry of history and culture that stretches back over a millennium, weaving together the threads of a storied past. This remarkable region, once the epicenter of England's wool trade, witnessed a flourishing of prosperity during the Middle Ages. The Cotswolds' rise to affluence is palpably etched in the very stones of its churches and manor houses, which punctuate the landscape with their majestic presence.

In the medieval heyday of the wool industry, the Cotswolds stood as a beacon of economic vitality, fueling trade and commerce throughout the region. This era saw the construction of grand edifices, each stone laid with precision and purpose. These architectural marvels, often adorned with intricate carvings and elegant stained glass, bear witness to the wealth and taste of the Cotswold's prosperous inhabitants.

The Cotswolds also bears the indelible marks of a tumultuous chapter in English history: the English Civil War. A conflict that pitted Royalists against Parliamentarians, it reverberated through the very heart of this picturesque countryside. The Cotswolds, due to its strategic importance, witnessed significant military activity during this time. Fortifications and battlegrounds, some of which still stand today, serve as silent sentinels to the strife that once engulfed the land.

Today, the Cotswolds stands as a living museum, where the echoes of the past reverberate through time. Immaculately preserved historical sites, from medieval market squares to Tudor-era manors, offer a captivating window into a bygone era. These sites bear witness to the architectural prowess and artistic endeavors of those who came before, their legacy etched in stone and timber.

Yet, the Cotswolds is not a mere relic of history. It is a living testament to the enduring spirit of its people. The region's vibrant arts and crafts scene, deeply rooted in tradition, breathes life into age-old practices. Artisans and craftsmen, inspired by the heritage that surrounds them, continue to create exquisite textiles, ceramics, and other handmade treasures. Visitors can explore studios and workshops, witnessing the meticulous craftsmanship that has been passed down through generations.

In every winding lane and hidden corner of the Cotswolds, the past and present intertwine seamlessly. The legacy of a thousand years is not consigned to the annals of history; it lives on in the very stones, in the stories told, and in the crafts that continue to flourish. The Cotswolds, with its rich tapestry of history and culture, invites visitors to step into a living, breathing museum, where the threads of the past are woven into the vibrant fabric of today. It is a testament to the enduring spirit of a region that has stood the test of time, leaving an indelible mark on all who have the privilege to walk its storied paths.

2.3 Languages and Communication

English stands as the predominant language in the Cotswolds, mirroring the linguistic landscape of the wider England. However, this captivating region's international allure has fostered a cultural diversity that extends to its linguistic fabric. Visitors will discover a warm and welcoming environment, where locals are adept at engaging with individuals who converse in an array of languages. In bustling tourist hubs, it's not uncommon to encounter residents proficient in French, German, Spanish, and other European languages.

Despite this linguistic versatility, a simple gesture, such as extending a friendly greeting or expressing gratitude in English, holds a universal charm that transcends language barriers. It resonates with an authenticity that is deeply appreciated by locals and fellow travelers alike. These small acts of courtesy bridge any gaps in language, forging connections that reflect the inclusive spirit of the Cotswolds. In this melting pot of cultures, communication takes on a delightful fluidity, enriching the travel experience for all who venture into this enchanting region. Whether in the heart of a bustling market town or amid the serenity of a rural hamlet, the language of hospitality speaks volumes, creating an atmosphere of camaraderie that transcends linguistic nuances. The Cotswolds, with its welcoming embrace and cultural diversity, exemplifies the beauty of shared experiences that extend far beyond the confines of spoken words.

2.4 Currency and Banking

The bedrock of financial transactions in the Cotswolds, as in the entirety of the United Kingdom, is the esteemed British Pound Sterling (£). This robust currency symbolizes a legacy steeped in history and is the preferred medium for all monetary exchanges in the region. To navigate the Cotswolds with ease, it's prudent to have a versatile approach to payment methods, combining both cash and cards.

While the majority of businesses in the Cotswolds readily accept major credit and debit cards, there is a prudent consideration to bear in mind. In the intimate nooks and crannies of this picturesque countryside, one may chance upon charming, family-run establishments that lean towards the traditional preference for cash transactions. This subtle preference, a nod to timeless customs, endows a distinctive character to the Cotswolds' local commerce.

For the convenience of travelers, Automated Teller Machines (ATMs) are thoughtfully scattered across towns and villages, ensuring effortless access to financial resources. These reliable machines stand as beacons of convenience, offering a hassle-free means to withdraw cash in the local currency. It's a prudent move to keep an eye out for these machines, particularly when venturing into more remote or less frequented corners of the Cotswolds.

Navigating the financial landscape of the Cotswolds, with its blend of modern convenience and traditional sensibilities, allows visitors to fully immerse themselves in the authentic experience of this idyllic region. Armed with a combination of British Pounds and plastic, travelers are poised to explore the charming markets, savor local delicacies, and indulge in the myriad cultural offerings that the Cotswolds so generously offers. This prudent mix ensures that every aspect of the journey, from quaint village shops to bustling market stalls, can be embraced with confidence and ease.

2.4.1 Currency Exchange Tips

Navigating currency exchange while exploring the Cotswolds is a matter of financial prudence that ensures a smooth and enriching travel experience. Here are some essential tips to consider:

1. Exchange Rates: Before engaging in any currency exchange, take a moment to check the prevailing exchange rates. Currency rates can fluctuate, so it's wise to be informed and compare your options to secure the best value for your money. This can help maximize your spending power during your journey through the Cotswolds.

2. Local Banks: In major towns throughout the Cotswolds, reputable banks stand ready to provide currency exchange

services. These establishments often offer competitive rates, making them a reliable choice for converting your currency. Local bank branches also provide the convenience of in-person assistance, ensuring a hassle-free exchange process.

3. Avoid Airport Exchanges: When arriving in the UK, it's advisable to steer clear of currency exchange services at airports. These facilities typically impose higher fees and offer less favorable exchange rates, which can erode the value of your money. Instead, opt to exchange your currency in town centers, where rates are typically more favorable, or conveniently withdraw cash from ATMs.

4. Notify Your Bank: If you plan to use your credit or debit cards while abroad, it's crucial to notify your bank or financial institution before embarking on your journey. Informing your bank of your travel plans helps prevent any unexpected disruptions in card service due to potential fraud alerts. This ensures that your financial transactions proceed seamlessly throughout your Cotswolds adventure.

5. Keep Small Denominations: While card payments are widely accepted in the Cotswolds, it's practical to carry some smaller denominations of local currency. This can be particularly handy for small purchases, such as souvenirs from local markets, or in situations where card payments may not be accepted, such as smaller, family-run businesses. Having small bills and coins on hand ensures you can effortlessly handle various spending scenarios, further enhancing your travel convenience.

By adhering to these currency exchange guidelines, you'll be well-prepared to navigate the financial landscape of the

Cotswolds with confidence. This ensures that you can focus on savoring the region's picturesque landscapes, cultural treasures, and culinary delights without any monetary worries along the way.

CHAPTER THREE

MUST VISIT DESTINATIONS

The Cotswolds are known for their picturesque villages, historic landmarks, and stunning natural beauty. Here are some must-visit destinations and sites for tourists exploring the Cotswolds:

3.1 Bibury:

Arlington Row: Iconic 17th-century Weaver's Cottages

Nestled in the heart of Bibury, Arlington Row stands as a timeless testament to the architectural heritage of the Cotswolds. This iconic row of 17th-century weaver's cottages, characterized by their distinctive honey-colored stone walls and steeply pitched roofs, exudes an enchanting charm that captures the imagination of all who encounter it.

Built in 1380 as a monastic wool store, Arlington Row underwent a transformation in the 17th century when it was converted into weaver's cottages. The cottages, with their picturesque appearance and idyllic setting along the banks of the River Coln, have become one of the most photographed and celebrated landmarks in the Cotswolds.

The architectural detail of Arlington Row is a testament to the craftsmanship of yesteryears. Each cottage features mullioned windows, stone-tiled roofs, and a series of gables that contribute to its distinctive character. As the sunlight dances on the Cotswold stone facades, it bestows a warm, golden glow that lends a magical aura to this historic site.

Visitors to Arlington Row have the opportunity to stroll along the quaint cobblestone pathway that runs alongside the cottages. This allows for an up-close appreciation of the intricate details and centuries-old craftsmanship that define this architectural gem. The verdant gardens that border the cottages further enhance the picturesque scene, creating a harmonious blend of natural beauty and historical significance.

Arlington Row's enduring appeal has not only made it a popular attraction for visitors but has also garnered recognition on a global scale. Its idyllic beauty has been featured in numerous films, paintings, and postcards, solidifying its status as an emblematic representation of the Cotswolds' quintessential charm.

For history enthusiasts, a visit to Arlington Row offers a captivating glimpse into the lives of weavers who once called these cottages home. The preserved interiors provide insight into the modest yet functional layout of 17th-century homes. Authentic period furnishings and artifacts offer a tangible connection to the past, allowing visitors to step back in time and envision the daily routines of those who resided within these walls.

In all seasons, Arlington Row exudes its own unique allure. Spring and summer bring vibrant blooms to the surrounding gardens, enhancing the picturesque setting with a riot of colors. Autumn bestows a warm, golden hue upon the Cotswold stone, creating a captivating contrast against the backdrop of changing foliage. Even in the quiet embrace of winter, the cottages exude a serene beauty, with frost-kissed gardens adding a touch of enchantment to the scene.

A visit to Arlington Row is a journey through time, a chance to witness the enduring legacy of craftsmanship and a celebration of the Cotswolds' timeless beauty. It stands as a living testament to the region's rich history and a tribute to the artisans who left their indelible mark on this enchanting corner of the world.

Bibury Trout Farm: Experience Fishing and See a Variety of Trout

Tucked away in the charming village of Bibury, the Bibury Trout Farm offers a unique and immersive experience for visitors of all ages. Established in 1902, this historic farm is not only one of the oldest working trout farms in England but also a place where nature, education, and recreation converge in perfect harmony.

The Bibury Trout Farm's idyllic setting along the tranquil waters of the River Coln provides a picturesque backdrop for an enriching day out. Upon arrival, visitors are greeted by a serene landscape of cascading pools and lush greenery, where the soothing sounds of flowing water create a calming atmosphere.

One of the main highlights of the farm is the opportunity to try your hand at fishing. Equipped with fishing rods and bait, visitors can cast their lines into the crystal-clear pools teeming with rainbow and brown trout. Whether you're an experienced angler or a novice seeking a new adventure, the farm provides an inviting environment for both skill levels.

For those looking to learn more about the lifecycle of these fascinating creatures, the Bibury Trout Farm offers guided tours that provide insight into the stages of trout development. From hatching and rearing to the eventual release into the farm's river, this educational experience offers a unique perspective on the conservation efforts undertaken by the farm.

The farm's dedicated staff are on hand to share their expertise and knowledge about trout farming and conservation. They offer informative demonstrations on fish handling and feeding, providing visitors with a deeper understanding of the farm's vital role in both local aquaculture and environmental preservation.

In addition to the interactive experiences, the Bibury Trout Farm features a charming shop where visitors can purchase freshly smoked and prepared trout, along with a selection of locally sourced produce and souvenirs. The shop serves as a delightful stop to savor the farm's produce or to take home a taste of the Cotswolds.

The Bibury Trout Farm is not only a place of leisure but also a hub of ecological awareness and conservation efforts. The farm's commitment to sustainable practices and responsible stewardship of the environment is evident in its dedication to maintaining the ecological balance of the river ecosystem.

For families, nature enthusiasts, and anyone seeking a tranquil escape, the Bibury Trout Farm offers an enriching experience that combines outdoor recreation with educational opportunities. It's a place where the beauty of nature and the rich tapestry of Cotswold heritage come together to create a memorable and meaningful visit for all who have the pleasure of exploring this cherished locale.

3.2 Castle Combe:

Castle Combe Village: A Quintessential Cotswold Village

Castle Combe Village is a true gem nestled amidst the undulating hills of the Cotswolds, presenting an enchanting tableau of England's rich heritage. Revered as one of the most captivating villages in the country, it transports visitors to a world steeped in timeless allure and pastoral tranquility.

Rooted in antiquity, Castle Combe's origins trace back to the Roman era, a history that echoes through its cobbled streets and weathered stones. The architectural symphony that graces the village is a marriage of honey-hued Cotswold stone and timber-framed cottages. This harmonious blend encapsulates the quintessence of rural England, each structure a silent sentinel of centuries gone by. As you wander its lanes, there's an undeniable sense that the very stones themselves hold the secrets of generations.

At the heart of Castle Combe stands the Market Cross, an ancient sentinel dating back to the 14th century. This ornate stone cross once served as the focal point for medieval commerce and communal gatherings. Today, it stands as a poignant relic, whispering tales of Castle Combe's vibrant history.

The gentle flow of the By Brook, meandering through the village, adds a lyrical cadence to the scene. Its presence bestows an ethereal quality upon Castle Combe, creating an atmosphere of tranquility that encourages quiet reflection and relaxation. The babbling brook becomes a soothing backdrop to the village's timeless beauty.

For cinephiles, Castle Combe holds a special place in cinematic annals. Its ethereal beauty has graced the screens in various film and television productions, solidifying its reputation as the quintessential English village. Notable among its appearances are in the film adaptation of "Doctor Doolittle" and the original production of "The War Horse". Castle Combe's enchanting backdrop provided the perfect canvas for these cinematic masterpieces, further immortalizing the village's timeless charm.

A leisurely amble through Castle Combe unfolds like turning the pages of a living storybook. Each corner reveals a new vista of enchanting architecture, gardens that burst with life, and hidden corners that beckon exploration. The village breathes an air of timelessness, where the centuries converge to weave a tapestry of beauty that transcends the boundaries of any single era.

As the sun bathes the village in a warm, golden glow, Castle Combe's magic is heightened. Each stone seems to resonate with a luminous energy, casting a spell that captivates the senses. The vibrant hues of blooming flora accentuate the village's innate beauty, creating a living portrait of pastoral perfection.

Castle Combe beckons visitors to lose themselves in its winding lanes, to pause and absorb the serenity of the moment. It is a place where the past lingers in every stone and the present is imbued with a sense of timelessness. In Castle Combe, the Cotswolds have bestowed a gift to the world, a village that serves as a portal to a world of enduring beauty and tranquility.

Manor House Hotel and Gardens: Stunning Historic Estate

Nestled within the embrace of Castle Combe village lies the Manor House Hotel, an opulent testament to centuries of English history and architectural grandeur. This stately manor, with its ivy-clad facade and imposing stone walls, stands as a sentinel of the past, offering visitors an unrivaled glimpse into the splendor of bygone eras.

Dating back to the 14th century, the Manor House Hotel is steeped in a rich tapestry of history. Once the residence of Sir John Fastolf, a knight who served as the inspiration for Shakespeare's character Falstaff, the estate exudes a palpable sense of regal heritage. The architecture seamlessly marries medieval and Tudor elements, showcasing a captivating blend of styles that have evolved over the centuries.

As you step into the grandeur of the Manor House, you are enveloped in a world of refined elegance and timeless luxury. The interior spaces boast intricately carved woodwork, ornate fireplaces, and exquisite period furnishings that pay homage to the estate's storied past. Each room is a testament to the craftsmanship and artistic sensibilities of the eras that have shaped this magnificent residence.

The Manor House Hotel also offers an indulgent culinary experience, where guests can savor the finest in English cuisine. The dining rooms, with their oak-paneled walls and beamed ceilings, provide an intimate setting for a gastronomic journey that celebrates the rich culinary traditions of the region.

One of the true jewels of the Manor House estate is its meticulously manicured gardens. Sprawling across acres of verdant terrain, the gardens are a sensory feast of color, fragrance, and tranquility. From the terraced lawns to the vibrant flowerbeds, every inch of the landscape is a testament to the artistry of the gardeners who have nurtured this natural masterpiece.

The gardens are a sanctuary of serenity, where guests can meander along winding paths, discover hidden alcoves, and bask in the beauty of nature's symphony. The bubbling of ornate fountains, the fragrance of blooming flora, and the song of birds create a harmonious symphony that elevates the experience to one of pure enchantment.

For guests seeking relaxation and rejuvenation, the Manor House Hotel offers a range of amenities, including a spa and wellness center. Here, amidst the tranquil setting of the Cotswolds, visitors can indulge in therapeutic treatments and wellness rituals that pamper the body and soothe the soul.

In every corner of the Manor House Hotel and its gardens, the echoes of history reverberate through time. It stands not only as a testament to architectural magnificence but also as a living canvas that showcases the evolution of English heritage. A visit to this splendid estate is an immersion into a world of refined elegance, where the past mingles seamlessly with the present, offering a glimpse into the enduring legacy of Castle Combe and the Cotswolds.

3.3 Bourton-on-the-Water:

Model Village: A Miniature Replica of the Village Itself

The Model Village of Castle Combe stands as a testament to the artistry of meticulous craftsmanship and a captivating showcase of architectural ingenuity. Nestled adjacent to the picturesque Castle Combe village, this miniature marvel offers a unique perspective on this idyllic Cotswold gem.

As visitors step into the Model Village, they are immediately transported into a world of enchanting diminutiveness. Every facet of Castle Combe is expertly recreated in astonishingly precise detail. The charming, honey-hued cottages, adorned with their distinctive timber beams, stand in perfect miniature, exuding the same character and allure as their full-sized counterparts. The cobbled streets wind through the village with a fidelity that is nothing short of remarkable, inviting exploration and evoking a sense of wonder.

The By Brook, a defining element of the Castle Combe landscape, is faithfully rendered in miniature form, mirroring its tranquil flow through the heart of the village. This miniature watercourse, complete with its own tiny bridges and embankments, emulates the natural rhythms of its full-sized counterpart. The careful attention to detail extends to the verdant foliage and meticulously manicured gardens that grace the model, recreating the lush beauty of Castle Combe's landscape.

The Model Village provides a fresh perspective on Castle Combe, inviting visitors to view this quintessential Cotswold village from a wholly unique vantage point. It offers an immersive experience that allows for a deeper appreciation of the architectural intricacies that define Castle Combe's charm. The opportunity to compare the model with the actual village itself adds a layer of fascination, highlighting the craftsmanship and artistry that have gone into its creation.

This scaled-down recreation is not merely a replica; it is a labor of love, a testament to the dedication and passion of those who brought it to life. The artisans behind the Model Village have left no stone unturned, meticulously recreating even the most minute details. Each tiny window, every miniature door, is crafted with precision and care, imbuing the model with a lifelike quality that is both awe-inspiring and delightful.

As visitors meander through the Model Village, they are invited to pause and soak in the whimsical beauty of this miniature world. It is a place where the boundaries between reality and imagination blur, where the art of craftsmanship merges seamlessly with the essence of a cherished village. The experience evokes a childlike wonder, as if one has stumbled upon a hidden world, waiting to be explored and admired.

The Model Village serves not only as a testament to artistic skill but also as a living homage to the enduring charm of Castle Combe. It offers a unique lens through which to view the village's timeless beauty, underscoring the architectural heritage that has made Castle Combe a beloved destination for generations. The model is a living tribute to the village it represents, a work of art that captures the very soul of Castle Combe in miniature form.

For visitors, the Model Village is an opportunity to engage with Castle Combe in a truly immersive way. It provides a deeper understanding of the village's layout, allowing one to trace the winding paths and discover hidden corners. It's a chance to appreciate the craftsmanship of its buildings up close, to marvel at the intricacies that make each cottage a work of art in itself.

In every nook and cranny of the Model Village, there is a sense of discovery, an invitation to lose oneself in the beauty of this meticulously crafted world. It is a place where imagination takes flight, where the spirit of Castle Combe is encapsulated in a miniature marvel. The Model Village is not just a recreation; it is a tribute, a testament, and a celebration of the enduring magic of Castle Combe, presented in a form that captivates the hearts and imaginations of all who have the privilege to experience it.

The Cotswold Motoring Museum: Vintage Cars and Memorabilia

The Cotswold Motoring Museum, nestled in the picturesque village of Bourton-on-the-Water, is a veritable haven for aficionados of automotive history and vintage vehicles. Stepping through its doors is like embarking on a captivating journey through the annals of motoring evolution.

The museum's collection reads like a chronicle of automotive heritage, with each meticulously restored vintage car serving as a testament to the craftsmanship and engineering prowess of its era. These vehicles, lovingly preserved and immaculately maintained, bear witness to the ingenuity that shaped the early days of motoring. From sleek, Art Deco-inspired designs to the robust elegance of pre-war classics, the museum's curated collection offers a panoramic view of automotive evolution.

Beyond the cars themselves, the museum is a treasure trove of motoring memorabilia. The exhibits are a vivid tapestry of period advertising, evocative signage, and an array of nostalgic artifacts that harken back to the golden age of automotive culture. Each piece tells a story, providing a window into the zeitgeist of the times when motoring was as much a cultural phenomenon as it was a mode of transportation. Vintage posters, enamel signs, and meticulously restored petrol pumps evoke a sense of nostalgia for an era defined by the allure of the open road.

As visitors wander through the museum's halls, they are surrounded by the sights and sounds of a bygone automotive era. The engines hum with a timeless resonance, capturing the essence of an age when motoring was a pursuit of both leisure and adventure. The craftsmanship of the vehicles is awe-inspiring, a testament to the dedication of those who have painstakingly preserved these automotive relics.

One of the museum's highlights is its dedication to capturing the essence of the British motor industry. From iconic marques like Austin, Morris, and MG to the luxury of Rolls-Royce and Bentley, the collection showcases the rich tapestry of British automotive history. Visitors can trace the lineage of these celebrated brands, from their early days of innovation to their enduring legacy in the automotive world.

The Cotswold Motoring Museum is more than a mere collection of cars; it is a living testament to the passion and dedication of those who have sought to preserve the heritage of motoring. Each vehicle is a labor of love, a tangible link to a bygone era. The museum's meticulous restoration work is a tribute to the artistry of the engineers and craftsmen who originally brought these vehicles to life.

For enthusiasts and casual visitors alike, the museum offers a deeply immersive experience. It's a journey through time, an opportunity to witness firsthand the evolution of automotive design, technology, and culture. The exhibits invite contemplation of the innovations that revolutionized transportation and changed the way we experience the world around us.

Moreover, the museum's location in the charming village of Bourton-on-the-Water adds an extra layer of allure. The tranquil ambiance of this quintessential Cotswold village serves as a fitting backdrop for an exploration of automotive history. The juxtaposition of vintage vehicles against the backdrop of the village's timeless beauty creates a uniquely enchanting atmosphere.

In the Cotswold Motoring Museum, visitors find themselves not only in the presence of historic vehicles but also in the midst of a living tribute to the pioneers of motoring. It is a place where the legacy of the open road is celebrated, where the spirit of adventure that defined early motoring is kept alive. The museum invites all who enter its doors to embark on a journey through time, to revel in the stories these vehicles tell, and to be inspired by the indomitable spirit of innovation that continues to drive the world of motoring forward.

3.4 Stow-on-the-Wold:

St. Edward's Church: A Historic Medieval Church

In the heart of Stow-on-the-Wold, a quaint market town nestled within the Cotswolds, stands the resplendent St. Edward's Church. This medieval marvel is a living testament to the rich tapestry of history woven throughout the region. With roots tracing back over a thousand years, the church is a revered icon of ecclesiastical architecture and a sacred sanctuary that has witnessed centuries of devotion.

The church's architecture is a captivating fusion of Norman and Gothic influences, a visual testament to the evolving architectural styles that have graced its venerable walls. The sturdy Norman nave, with its robust pillars and rounded arches, harks back to an era of architectural austerity and functional elegance. As one ventures further into the church, the soaring Gothic arches and delicate tracery of the chancel evoke a sense of ethereal grace, characteristic of the later medieval period.

One of the most striking features of St. Edward's is its elegant and slender spire, which pierces the sky with a graceful ascent. This pinnacle of architectural achievement stands as a beacon, visible from afar, and a symbol of spiritual aspiration. The spire serves as a reminder of the profound impact that such architectural masterpieces had on the landscape and the communities they served.

Within the hallowed confines of St. Edward's, the play of light and shadow casts an enchanting aura over the ancient stone. Stained glass windows, their vibrant hues telling stories of faith and devotion, dapple the interior with a kaleidoscope of colors. Each pane is a work of art in itself, a testament to the skill and dedication of the artisans who crafted them. The interplay of light and glass creates a transcendent atmosphere, inviting contemplation and reverence.

The church's interior is adorned with an array of historic artifacts, including intricately carved wooden screens, centuries-old brasses, and ancient tombs that bear the weight of time. Each element is a chapter in the story of St. Edward's, offering a tangible connection to the generations who have sought solace within these sacred walls. The sense of continuity, of being part of an unbroken chain of worship and tradition, permeates the very air.

Beyond its architectural and artistic splendor, St. Edward's Church is a living hub of community life. It has borne witness to countless baptisms, weddings, and funerals, marking the milestones of generations past. The echoes of hymns sung and prayers offered resonate through the ages, creating a spiritual resonance that transcends time itself.

The churchyard, with its ancient gravestones and weathered memorials, is a serene oasis of contemplation. Here, beneath the whispering boughs of ancient yew trees, the departed rest in eternal repose, their stories etched in the epitaphs that adorn their final resting places. It is a place of quiet reflection, where the cycles of life and death are woven into the very fabric of the landscape.

Market Square: Traditional Market Town Atmosphere

As the heart and soul of Stow-on-the-Wold, the Market Square is a living testament to the enduring vitality of traditional market town life. Stepping into this bustling epicenter is like stepping back in time, where the echoes of centuries-old commerce still reverberate through the cobbled streets.

The square itself is framed by a picturesque tableau of historic buildings, their facades adorned with mellowed Cotswold stone. Time-worn timbers and charming dormer windows tell stories of centuries past, evoking a sense of nostalgia for an era when market towns were the lifeblood of local communities.

On market days, the square comes alive with a vibrant tapestry of stalls and vendors. The air is infused with the scent of freshly baked bread, the cheerful chatter of traders, and the delighted exclamations of visitors exploring the wares on offer. From artisanal crafts to locally sourced produce, the market offers a diverse array of goods, each a testament to the skill and creativity of local artisans.

The market's legacy stretches back through the annals of time, harkening to an age when such gatherings were not only hubs of trade but also centers of social interaction and community cohesion. In this historic square, the rhythms of life follow the same age-old cadence that has defined market towns for generations.

Surrounding the square are a wealth of charming shops, boutiques, and eateries. Each storefront bears the distinctive character of the Cotswolds, offering a curated selection of goods that celebrate the region's heritage and craftsmanship. From bespoke antiques to handcrafted jewelry, the offerings are a testament to the enduring tradition of skilled artisans who call this corner of the world home.

Amidst the market day bustle, the ancient market cross stands as a sentinel, a silent witness to centuries of commerce and community. Its weathered stones and graceful arches are a poignant reminder of the enduring legacy of market towns, where the exchange of goods and ideas has been the lifeblood of local culture.

In the evening, as the day's activities wind down, the Market Square takes on a different kind of magic. The soft glow of lamplight bathes the cobbled streets in a warm, inviting radiance. The buildings, now bathed in a tranquil twilight, exude a timeless elegance that invites quiet contemplation.

For visitors, the Market Square is more than a place of commerce; it is a living tableau of tradition and community. It is a place where the past seamlessly intertwines with the present, where the rhythms of market life continue to beat in harmony with the modern world. It is a place to wander, to explore, and to immerse oneself in the rich tapestry of Cotswold heritage that unfolds in every corner of this charming square.

3.5 Chipping Campden:

High Street: Lined with charming honey-colored buildings.

The High Street of Chipping Campden unfurls like a storybook, its cobbled path winding through a tableau of enchanting honey-colored buildings. This quintessential thoroughfare stands as a living testament to the timeless allure of the Cotswolds, where history, architecture, and community converge in a symphony of charm.

As one steps onto the High Street, the first thing that captivates is the warm, golden hue that bathes the buildings. Crafted from the distinctive Cotswold stone, each facade exudes a sense of ageless elegance. The stone, with its mellowed tones, holds within its grains the echoes of centuries past. It tells tales of artisans and craftsmen, whose hands shaped these structures with care and precision. The interplay of light upon the weathered stone creates a visual spectacle, casting the street in a soft, golden glow that enchants both visitors and locals alike.

Wandering along the High Street is akin to embarking on a journey through time. The buildings, some bearing the weight of six centuries, stand as silent sentinels to the passage of history. Their timeworn timbers and leaning facades impart a sense of history that permeates the very air. Each leaning beam and slightly uneven doorway tells a story of centuries of habitation, of families and individuals who have called these buildings home. It is a place where the past mingles seamlessly with the present, where each step is a stride through centuries of tradition and heritage.

The High Street is more than a thoroughfare; it is a living testament to the spirit of community. The shops that line its cobbled expanse are a treasure trove of artisanal wares, boutique finds, and locally crafted goods. From bespoke jewelry to hand-painted ceramics, each storefront offers a curated selection of treasures that celebrate the creativity and talent of the Cotswolds' artisans. These establishments are more than places of commerce; they are the heartbeats of a community, where passionate artisans share their craft with a world eager to experience their unique creations.

At the heart of the High Street stands the ancient Market Hall, a distinctive two-story structure with its timber-framed facade. This historic edifice, built in the early 17th century, served as a hub of commerce and community gatherings. Its elevated upper floor, supported by sturdy wooden columns, once provided a covered space for traders to display their wares. Today, the Market Hall stands as a poignant reminder of the market town's enduring legacy as a center of trade and social interaction. It is a living link to the past, a structure that has borne witness to generations of market days and community celebrations.

The High Street is not merely a place to pass through, but a destination in itself. It invites leisurely strolls, with every corner turned revealing a new vista of architectural splendor. The nooks and crannies that beckon exploration are brimming with hidden gems, from charming courtyards to secret gardens, each offering a glimpse into the intimate beauty that lies just beyond the main thoroughfare. These hidden enclaves are like whispered secrets, known to those who take the time to explore, and they add an extra layer of enchantment to the High Street experience.

As the seasons change, so too does the character of the High Street. In spring, trailing wisteria and blossoming flowers adorn the facades, infusing the air with the sweet fragrance of nature's rebirth. In summer, the street comes alive with vibrant window displays and bustling cafes, where visitors can pause to savor the delights of local cuisine. Autumn brings a rich tapestry of colors, as the leaves of ancient trees that line the street turn to gold and russet, creating a scene of natural splendor.

In winter, the High Street takes on a cozy intimacy, with the warm glow of shop windows inviting visitors to step inside and escape the chill. Festive decorations adorn the facades, casting a merry ambiance over the street. The sound of carolers and the scent of mulled wine infuse the air with a holiday spirit that warms the heart.

For residents, the High Street is more than a place of commerce; it is a living extension of home. It is a place to gather, to chat with neighbors, and to savor the simple pleasures of daily life. The familiar facades of the buildings become like old friends, their presence a comforting backdrop to the ebb and flow of everyday routines. They are witnesses to the comings and goings of generations, standing as steadfast guardians of the town's heritage.

In the High Street of Chipping Campden, the spirit of the Cotswolds comes alive. It is a place where history and modernity harmonize, where the traditions of the past are woven into the fabric of daily life. It is a thoroughfare of enchantment, where each step is a journey through centuries of architectural splendor and communal spirit. It is a living testament to the enduring beauty and spirit of the Cotswolds, a place where the past and present converge in a celebration of heritage and community.

Hidcote Manor Garden: One of the most famous gardens in England.

Nestled in the heart of the Cotswolds, Hidcote Manor Garden stands as a living masterpiece, a testament to the artistry and vision of its creator, Lawrence Johnston. Regarded as one of the most famous gardens in England, Hidcote is a horticultural jewel that has captured the hearts and imaginations of visitors from around the world.

The garden's story unfolds like a tapestry of creativity and passion. In the early 20th century, Lawrence Johnston, an American-born horticulturist, acquired Hidcote Manor and embarked on a lifelong journey to transform the grounds into a horticultural haven. Drawing inspiration from his travels and a keen sense of design, Johnston set about creating a series of interconnected outdoor "rooms," each with its own distinct character and theme.

As visitors step into Hidcote, they are immediately enveloped in a sensory symphony. The air is alive with the fragrances of blooming flowers and the earthy scent of foliage. The sound of rustling leaves and chirping birds provides a gentle, natural soundtrack to the garden's tranquil ambiance. Every step along the meticulously laid pathways reveals a new vista of botanical wonder, a testament to Johnston's meticulous planning and keen eye for detail.

The garden's architectural bones are defined by a series of intricately designed hedges, walls, and trellises. These elements not only serve as structural backdrops but also as living canvases for a diverse array of plants. Johnston's careful selection of species, often sourced from around the globe, reflects his deep understanding of horticulture and his desire to create a garden that would thrive in the Cotswold climate.

One of Hidcote's defining features is its series of "garden rooms," each with its own distinct theme and planting scheme. These rooms unfold in a carefully choreographed sequence, inviting visitors on a journey of discovery. From the exuberant colors of the Red Borders to the serene tranquility of the Bathing Pool Garden, each room offers a unique sensory experience.

The Old Garden, with its historic stone walls and classical statuary, exudes a timeless elegance. Here, heritage roses climb ancient stone structures, their blossoms infusing the air with a sweet, nostalgic perfume. The White Garden, awash in an ethereal palette of white and green, offers a serene respite, a place of quiet contemplation amidst billowing blooms and verdant foliage.

In contrast, the Fuchsia Garden explodes in a riot of magenta and purple, a vibrant celebration of color that dances in the dappled sunlight. The Pillar Garden, with its carefully trained topiaries and meticulously clipped hedges, exudes a sense of formal grandeur, a nod to classic garden design.

Beyond its aesthetic beauty, Hidcote Manor Garden is a living canvas of horticultural innovation. Johnston's experiments with plant combinations and his keen understanding of microclimates have left a legacy that continues to inspire gardeners and horticulturists to this day. The garden's diverse collection of flora, from rare and exotic specimens to tried-and-true classics, showcases the breadth and depth of Johnston's botanical knowledge.

As the seasons ebb and flow, Hidcote Manor Garden undergoes a transformation that is nothing short of magical. Spring heralds a riot of color as bulbs burst forth in a symphony of blooms. Summer brings a lush abundance, with perennials and shrubs vying for attention in a vibrant tapestry of foliage and flowers. Autumn casts its golden spell, as the garden's foliage takes on hues of russet and amber, creating a scene of breathtaking beauty.

Winter reveals a different kind of enchantment, as the garden's structural elements come to the forefront. The intricate silhouettes of hedges and topiaries are revealed, their forms etched against the winter sky. The garden's evergreen backbone provides a sense of continuity, reminding visitors that even in dormancy, Hidcote exudes an enduring beauty.

For visitors, Hidcote Manor Garden is a place of inspiration and reflection. It is a canvas of ever-changing beauty, a testament to the inexhaustible creativity of the natural world. It is a place to wander, to pause, and to be immersed in the timeless beauty of the Cotswolds. Each visit reveals new nuances, new combinations, and new perspectives, inviting a deeper appreciation for the intricate dance of life that unfolds within this horticultural masterpiece.

Hidcote Manor Garden transcends mere aesthetics; it is a living work of art that speaks to the soul. It is a testament to the transformative power of nature and the boundless creativity of those who tend to its embrace. It is a sanctuary of beauty and a celebration of the enduring magic that gardens, at their best, offer to the world.

3.6 Blenheim Palace (nearby in Woodstock):

Nestled within the heart of Oxfordshire, Blenheim Palace is a living testament to the grandeur and historical significance of British architecture. It stands as a UNESCO World Heritage Site, a testament to the enduring legacy of its creator, John Churchill, the first Duke of Marlborough. Beyond its architectural splendor, Blenheim holds a unique place in history as the birthplace of one of Britain's most iconic leaders, Sir Winston Churchill.

The palace's architectural magnificence is a harmonious blend of Baroque and English Palladian styles. Conceived by Sir John Vanbrugh, a celebrated architect of his time, and Nicholas Hawksmoor, the palace exudes an opulence that reflects the political and social stature of the Churchill family. The monumental façade, with its Corinthian columns and commanding presence, is a testament to the grand ambitions of its creators.

The interiors of Blenheim Palace are a feast for the senses, a showcase of artistry and craftsmanship. Ornate stucco work adorns the ceilings, intricate woodwork graces the walls, and opulent tapestries tell stories of dynastic triumphs. The Great Hall, with its soaring height and gilded detailing, sets a tone of regal splendor. The State Rooms, resplendent in their period furnishings and art collections, offer a glimpse into the refined tastes of generations past.

The palace's opulent interiors are complemented by the breathtaking beauty of its surrounding gardens and parkland. Lancelot "Capability" Brown, one of the foremost landscape architects of the 18th century, crafted the park into a natural masterpiece. The serene lake, sweeping lawns, and strategically placed groves create a harmonious fusion of nature and artifice. As visitors stroll through the meticulously designed grounds, they are enveloped in a sense of tranquility that belies the scale and ambition of the landscape.

One of the most iconic features of the park is the Grand Bridge, an architectural marvel that spans the lake. Its graceful arches and classical design serve not only as a functional structure but also as a visual focal point, framing picturesque vistas of the palace and the surrounding landscape. The bridge is a testament to the artistry and engineering prowess of its era, a symbol of the marriage of aesthetics and functionality that defines Blenheim.

Beyond its architectural and horticultural splendor, Blenheim Palace holds a special place in the annals of history as the birthplace of Sir Winston Churchill. The great statesman and leader of World War II spent his formative years within the hallowed halls of Blenheim, and the palace stands as a living tribute to his enduring legacy. The Churchill Exhibition within the palace provides a poignant insight into the life and times of this remarkable figure, showcasing personal mementos, documents, and photographs that offer a glimpse into the man behind the legend.

The gardens surrounding Blenheim Palace are a testament to the enduring allure of horticulture. The Formal Gardens, with their geometric precision and vibrant flowerbeds, offer a stark contrast to the sweeping natural landscapes. The Water Terraces, with their cascading fountains and sculpted statues, create a sense of refined elegance. The Rose Garden, a riot of color and fragrance, invites visitors to immerse themselves in a sensory symphony.

As visitors explore the gardens, they are met with a diverse array of plantings, from rare and exotic species to carefully curated collections of roses, azaleas, and ornamental shrubs. The Water Garden, with its serene pools and lush vegetation, offers a tranquil oasis for reflection. The Walled Garden, with its productive beds and meticulously maintained espaliered fruit trees, pays homage to the historic tradition of kitchen gardens.

Blenheim Palace and Gardens are more than a static monument to history; they are a living, breathing testament to the enduring power of art, architecture, and horticulture. Each visit reveals new nuances, new perspectives, and new layers of appreciation for the artistry and craftsmanship that define this extraordinary estate.

The palace and its grounds serve as a cultural beacon, hosting a diverse array of events and exhibitions throughout the year. From art installations to literary festivals, Blenheim Palace is a dynamic canvas that invites contemporary artists and creators to engage with its storied past.

For visitors, Blenheim is not merely a place to visit, but an experience to be savored. It is a journey through history, a celebration of artistic achievement, and a tribute to the indomitable spirit of Sir Winston Churchill. It is a place where the grandeur of the past converges with the vitality of the present, inviting all who enter to be transported by its beauty and inspired by its legacy.

3.7 Sudeley Castle (near Winchcombe):

In the heart of the Cotswolds, a region steeped in history and natural splendor, lies a jewel of both architectural and horticultural magnificence—a historic castle and its resplendent gardens. This cherished site, with its regal connections and enduring legacy, stands as a living testament to the grandeur and cultural significance that defines the Cotswolds.

The castle, a formidable edifice that has withstood the test of time, bears witness to centuries of history. Its imposing walls and towers rise majestically, a sentinel against the backdrop of the surrounding landscape. The architecture is a testament to the craftsmanship and engineering prowess of the eras that contributed to its construction. From the robust Norman keeps to the graceful turrets and battlements added in later centuries, the castle is a visual symphony that weaves together various architectural styles, reflecting the evolution of defensive structures over time.

Within the castle's storied walls lies a treasure trove of history. The Great Hall, with its soaring timbered roof and grand fireplace, is a space that once hosted feasts, celebrations, and the gatherings of nobility. Its walls bear witness to the echoes of laughter, the clinking of goblets, and the exchange of ideas that shaped the course of history. The castle's State Rooms, resplendent in their period furnishings and priceless artworks, offer a glimpse into the lives and lifestyles of generations of nobility. Each room is a canvas of history, a snapshot frozen in time, where the tapestries, portraits, and artifacts speak volumes about the culture and society of their respective eras.

The castle's connection to royalty adds a layer of significance to its legacy. It has been a place of refuge and residence for monarchs, a backdrop to momentous events, and a testament to the enduring bond between the crown and the Cotswolds. The chambers once graced by kings and queens, the halls where royal proclamations were made, and the battlements that provided strategic vantage points—all bear the weight of royal history.

The gardens surrounding the castle are a breathtaking complement to its architectural splendor. They have been sculpted and cultivated over centuries, evolving to reflect the changing tastes and horticultural trends of their times. From meticulously designed formal gardens to wild, romantic landscapes, the gardens are a testament to the creativity and vision of generations of gardeners.

One of the most iconic features of the gardens is the Rose Garden, a riot of color and fragrance that delights the senses. Here, rows of meticulously tended roses burst forth in a kaleidoscope of hues, creating a sensory symphony that captivates visitors. The carefully selected varieties, each chosen for its beauty and fragrance, create a vibrant tapestry that pays homage to the age-old tradition of cultivating these cherished blooms.

Beyond the formal gardens, the landscape unfolds in a series of natural vignettes. The Woodland Walk, with its dappled sunlight and meandering pathways, invites visitors to immerse themselves in a tranquil oasis of nature. The Herbaceous Borders, with their exuberant profusion of flowering plants, provide a vibrant counterpoint to the formal geometry of the gardens.

One cannot overlook the significance of water in the design of the gardens. The presence of ponds, streams, and fountains creates a dynamic interplay between the natural elements and the meticulously crafted landscape. Water features, such as cascades and ornamental pools, add a sense of movement and vitality to the gardens, inviting contemplation and reflection.

The gardens also serve as a living canvas for contemporary artists and sculptors. Temporary installations and exhibitions breathe new life into the landscape, offering visitors a fresh perspective on the intersection of art and nature. These artistic interventions add an extra layer of dynamism to the gardens, ensuring that each visit is a unique experience.

For visitors, the castle and its gardens are a journey through time, a passage through the annals of history and horticulture. They are a canvas of beauty, a celebration of cultural heritage, and a testament to the enduring appeal of the Cotswolds. Each step through the castle's halls and gardens reveals new layers of appreciation for the craftsmanship, creativity, and dedication that have shaped this remarkable site.

The castle and its gardens are not merely a static monument to history, but a living, breathing testament to the power of human ingenuity and artistic expression. They invite visitors to be transported by their beauty, inspired by their legacy, and immersed in the rich tapestry of the Cotswolds' cultural heritage. They are a testament to the enduring allure of this remarkable region, where the past converges with the present in a celebration of history, art, and nature.

3.8 Cotswold Way (Scenic Trail):

Nestled within the idyllic landscape of the Cotswolds lies a treasure trove of natural beauty and serenity—an area that offers not only stunning vistas but also a network of picturesque walking routes that beckon adventurers and nature enthusiasts alike. This enchanting region, with its rolling hills, meandering streams, and charming villages, is a veritable paradise for those seeking to immerse themselves in the timeless allure of the English countryside.

The Cotswolds' undulating hills, cloaked in a patchwork quilt of green fields, are a defining feature of the landscape. These gentle giants, carved by millennia of geological processes, offer panoramic views that stretch as far as the eye can see. From vantage points atop these hills, visitors are treated to a visual feast of boundless horizons, where the interplay of light and shadow creates an ever-changing tapestry of natural splendor.

One such vantage point that captures the essence of the Cotswolds is Dover's Hill. Perched atop the northern escarpment, this elevated vantage point offers a commanding view of the surrounding countryside. As visitors stand on the crest of the hill, they are greeted by a vista that unfolds like a living painting—the verdant fields, quaint villages, and distant woodlands create a scene of timeless beauty. It is a place where the elements converge in a symphony of color and form, inviting contemplation and appreciation.

The Cotswold Way, a designated National Trail, weaves its way through the heart of this captivating region, offering a network of walking routes that showcase the very best of the Cotswolds' natural splendor. This well-marked trail invites adventurers on a journey that spans over a hundred miles, leading them through a diverse array of landscapes, from open meadows to ancient woodlands. Along the way, walkers encounter charming villages, historic sites, and, of course, breathtaking views.

The picturesque village of Broadway, often referred to as the "Jewel of the Cotswolds," serves as a gateway to the Cotswold Way. As walkers set forth from this quintessential English village, they embark on a journey that traverses some of the most scenic stretches of the trail. The climb to Broadway Tower, an iconic folly perched on the edge of the escarpment, rewards hikers with an unparalleled view that stretches over the Vale of Evesham, a patchwork of orchards and farmland.

As the trail winds its way through the countryside, it meanders through ancient beech woodlands, where dappled sunlight filters through the canopy, casting a gentle glow on the forest floor. The scent of moss and earth mingles in the air, creating a sensory experience that connects walkers with the natural world.

The Cotswold Way also offers the opportunity to explore the timeless charm of Cotswold villages. From the honey-hued stone cottages of Stanton to the bustling market town of Winchcombe, each settlement along the way has its own unique character and history. The trails that lead through these villages are like threads in a tapestry, weaving together the rich cultural heritage of the Cotswolds.

One of the most enchanting aspects of walking in the Cotswolds is the sense of tranquility and seclusion that can be found, even in the midst of such natural beauty. There are moments when the only sounds are the rustling of leaves, the chirping of birds, and the distant flow of a stream. It is a place where one can find solace in the embrace of nature, where the worries and cares of the world seem to fade away.

As the seasons paint their colors across the landscape, the Cotswolds undergoes a transformation that is nothing short of magical. In spring, the hedgerows burst forth in a riot of blossoms, and the fields are ablaze with wildflowers. Summer brings the heady scent of blooming roses and the vibrant hues of butterfly wings. Autumn casts its golden spell, as the leaves of ancient trees turn to shades of amber and russet, creating a scene of breathtaking beauty.

In winter, the landscape takes on a quiet elegance, with frost-covered fields and bare branches etched against the pale sky. The Cotswolds' timeless beauty knows no season, and each time of year brings its own unique enchantment.

For walkers and nature enthusiasts, the Cotswolds offers not only stunning views but also an invitation to embark on a journey through an ever-changing landscape of natural beauty. It is a place where the soul finds solace, where the senses are awakened, and where the wonders of the natural world unfold in a symphony of color and form. It is a region that calls out to be explored, to be savored, and to be cherished for generations to come.

3.9 Broadway Tower:

In the heart of England's picturesque Cotswolds, where the landscape unfurls in a tapestry of rolling hills, ancient woodlands, and charming villages, there exist vantage points that gift visitors with an awe-inspiring panorama of this timeless countryside. These elevated perspectives, where the eye can drink in the boundless beauty of the Cotswolds, are like windows into a world of natural splendor that captivates the soul.

Dover's Hill, a prominent vantage point situated on the northern edge of the Cotswold escarpment, stands as an emblematic site that encapsulates the grandeur of the region. As one stands atop this commanding hill, the vista that unfolds is nothing short of spectacular. The Cotswolds stretch out before you, a patchwork quilt of green fields, quaint villages, and undulating hills that seem to ripple into the horizon. It is a view that transcends time, inviting contemplation and a deep appreciation for the beauty of the natural world.

From Dover's Hill, the eye is drawn across the Vale of Evesham, where orchards and farmland extend like a lush carpet, punctuated by the occasional hamlet or market town. The River Avon meanders through the landscape, its shimmering ribbon of water adding a touch of serenity to the scene. The play of light and shadow on the fields creates a dynamic interplay of color and form, an ever-changing tableau that captivates the senses.

The Cotswold Way, a renowned National Trail that traverses the region, offers a network of walking routes that lead to these panoramic viewpoints. Stretching over a hundred miles, the trail weaves its way through a diverse tapestry of landscapes, from open meadows to ancient woodlands. Along the way, walkers are treated to a succession of breathtaking views that showcase the Cotswolds in all its natural splendor.

The village of Broadway, often referred to as the "Jewel of the Cotswolds," serves as a gateway to the Cotswold Way. From here, walkers embark on a journey that leads them to some of the most scenic stretches of the trail. The ascent to Broadway Tower, a historic folly perched on the edge of the escarpment, is a highlight of the route. As visitors reach the summit, they are rewarded with a view that spans over the Vale of Evesham, a patchwork of orchards and farmland that extends to the distant horizon.

Broadway Tower itself is a historic landmark, with a rich history that dates back to the late 18th century. Its construction was inspired by the architectural designs of Capability Brown and James Wyatt, who sought to create a structure that would both complement the landscape and serve as a beacon for visitors. Today, the tower stands as a testament to their vision, offering visitors a unique opportunity to ascend its heights and take in the unparalleled view.

The Woodland Walk, a segment of the Cotswold Way, invites walkers to immerse themselves in the tranquil embrace of ancient beech woodlands. Here, the forest canopy creates a cathedral-like atmosphere, where dappled sunlight filters through the leaves, casting a gentle glow on the forest floor. The scent of moss and earth permeates the air, creating a sensory experience that connects walkers with the natural world.

As walkers tread the pathways of the Cotswold Way, they encounter a tapestry of landscapes, each with its own unique character and charm. The trail leads through quaint villages, where honey-colored stone cottages nestle amidst vibrant gardens. It winds through open fields, where sheep graze and wildflowers sway in the breeze. It meanders along the edges of woodlands, where ancient trees stand as silent sentinels to the passage of time.

One cannot help but be struck by the sense of seclusion and tranquility that pervades these natural spaces. In the embrace of the Cotswolds countryside, there are moments when the only sounds are the rustling of leaves, the chirping of birds, and the gentle whisper of the wind. It is a place where one can find solace and renewal, where the cares of the world seem to fade away.

As the seasons paint their colors across the landscape, the Cotswolds undergoes a transformation that is nothing short of magical. In spring, the hedgerows burst forth in a riot of blossoms, and the fields are ablaze with wildflowers. Summer brings the heady scent of blooming roses and the vibrant hues of butterfly wings. Autumn casts its golden spell, as the leaves of ancient trees turn to shades of amber and russet, creating a scene of breathtaking beauty.

In winter, the landscape takes on a quiet elegance, with frost-covered fields and bare branches etched against the pale sky. The Cotswolds' timeless beauty knows no season, and each time of year brings its own unique enchantment.

For those who venture forth to these panoramic viewpoints, the Cotswolds offers not only stunning vistas but also an invitation to immerse oneself in the grandeur and tranquility of the natural world. It is a place where the soul finds solace, where the senses are awakened, and where the wonders of nature unfold in a symphony of color and form. It is a region that calls out to be explored, to be savored, and to be cherished for generations to come. The panoramic views of the Cotswolds countryside are not merely scenes to be admired; they are experiences that linger in the memory, reminders of the enduring beauty that graces this remarkable region.

3.10 The Rollright Stones:

Nestled within the heart of the Cotswolds lies a place steeped in ancient mystery and folklore—an enigmatic site known as the Rollright Stones. This megalithic complex, comprised of three distinct formations—the King's Men, the Whispering Knights, and the King Stone—stands as a testament to the enduring connection between humanity and the natural world. It is a place where the echoes of ancient rituals and beliefs reverberate through the ages, inviting visitors on a mystical journey through time.

The Rollright Stones are believed to have origins dating back over five millennia, to the Late Neolithic and Early Bronze Age periods. This remarkable timeline places them within the realm of prehistory, a time when early human communities lived in harmony with the land, and the natural world held profound spiritual significance.

The King's Men, the most prominent and visually striking of the three formations, is a circle of seventy-seven weathered stones, each with its own unique character and presence. They stand sentinel-like, their rugged surfaces bearing the marks of countless centuries. This stone circle, measuring approximately one hundred feet in diameter, exudes a sense of timelessness, as if it has borne witness to the ebb and flow of millennia.

Legend has it that the stones are the petrified remains of a group of rebellious warriors, who were turned to stone by a witch or a powerful sorcerer. Their transformation, a punishment for their defiance, has left them frozen in their final act of defiance, forever immortalized in stone. This tale, woven from the threads of folklore and imagination, adds a layer of mystique to the site, inviting visitors to ponder the stories that lie beneath the surface.

Adjacent to the King's Men lies the Whispering Knights, a cluster of five upright stones that stand in close proximity to one another. Their placement, like ancient sentinels in conversation, creates an intimate circle within the larger landscape. The origin of their name is steeped in folklore, suggesting that the stones were conspiring in hushed tones, perhaps plotting a nefarious deed or sharing secrets lost to the annals of time.

The King Stone, standing apart from the others, is a solitary sentinel that commands attention with its imposing presence. It is believed to represent a chieftain or leader, and its solitary stature evokes a sense of reverence and authority. The stone, positioned to overlook the rest of the complex, seems to preside over the site, a symbolic figurehead that watches over the ancient landscape.

The Rollright Stones, like many megalithic sites, are aligned with celestial phenomena, adding a layer of astronomical significance to their ancient purpose. The stones' positioning, with a clear view of the horizon, suggests an awareness of the cyclical movements of the sun, moon, and stars. This cosmic alignment may have played a role in the rituals and ceremonies conducted at the site, allowing early inhabitants to mark the passage of time and the changing of seasons.

The Rollright Stones have long been a site of pilgrimage, drawing visitors from near and far who seek to connect with the ancient energies that permeate the landscape. For some, the stones hold a profound spiritual significance, serving as a place of meditation, reflection, and communion with the natural world. Others are drawn by a sense of curiosity and a desire to unravel the mysteries that enshroud the site.

The stones' enduring appeal is a testament to their ability to transcend the boundaries of time and culture, resonating with a diverse array of individuals who find solace and inspiration within their ancient embrace. Whether viewed through the lens of archaeology, folklore, or spirituality, the Rollright Stones continue to captivate the imagination and stir the soul.

Surrounding the stones is a landscape of pastoral beauty, where meadows stretch out beneath open skies and the gentle undulations of the Cotswold hills provide a fitting backdrop to this ancient site. The surrounding flora and fauna, from wildflowers that carpet the fields in spring to the rustling leaves of ancient trees, contribute to the timeless ambiance that permeates the Rollright Stones.

As the seasons paint their colors across the landscape, the Rollright Stones undergo a transformation that is nothing short of magical. In spring, the meadows burst forth in a riot of blossoms, and the air is alive with the hum of pollinators. Summer brings the heady scent of wildflowers and the vibrant hues of butterfly wings. Autumn casts its golden spell, as the leaves of ancient trees turn to shades of amber and russet, creating a scene of breathtaking beauty.

In winter, the landscape takes on a quiet elegance, with frost-kissed grasses and the sculptural silhouettes of bare trees etched against the winter sky. The stones, weathered and enduring, stand as silent sentinels to the passage of time. The Rollright Stones' timeless beauty knows no season, and each time of year brings its own unique enchantment.

For those who venture to the Rollright Stones, it is not merely a visit to a historical site, but a journey through time and a communion with the ancient energies that have shaped this remarkable place. It is an opportunity to stand in the footsteps of those who came before, to touch the weathered surface of stones that have borne witness to the passage of millennia.

It is a chance to experience the sense of wonder and reverence that accompanies the exploration of ancient sites, where the line between the past and the present blurs, and the mysteries of history beckon to be unraveled. The Rollright Stones are not merely stones; they are gateways to a deeper understanding of our shared human heritage and a reminder of the enduring connections that bind us to the natural world. They are a living testament to the power of ancient sites to inspire, to captivate, and to awaken the imagination.

3.11 Westonbirt Arboretum (near Tetbury):

Nestled on the outskirts of the picturesque town of Tetbury in the heart of the Cotswolds lies a horticultural gem—a place of boundless natural beauty and biodiversity known as the Westonbirt Arboretum. This living testament to the world of trees is a sanctuary for both native and exotic species, a place where the artistry of nature is on full display. It invites visitors on a journey through a verdant tapestry of botanical splendor, where each season brings new colors, scents, and textures to delight the senses.

Spanning over 600 acres, the arboretum is a meticulously curated collection of trees and shrubs, carefully selected from around the globe. Its creation can be traced back to the early 19th century, when Robert Stayner Holford, a visionary landowner with a passion for horticulture, embarked on the ambitious project of establishing an arboretum on his estate. Over the years, successive generations of dedicated horticulturists and arborists have contributed to the expansion and enrichment of this arboreal haven.

The arboretum is a living encyclopedia of tree species, showcasing over 15,000 individual specimens representing around 2,500 different types. From towering giants to delicate ornamentals, each tree tells a story of its native habitat, ecological significance, and cultural importance. Visitors can embark on a journey around the world without leaving the Cotswolds, encountering species from North America, Asia, Europe, and beyond.

One of the arboretum's most celebrated features is the Silk Wood, a vast expanse of ancient woodland that forms the heart of this botanical sanctuary. This woodland, with its centuries-old trees and rich understorey of shrubs and wildflowers, offers a glimpse into the natural heritage of the region. Here, ancient oaks, beeches, and chestnuts tower overhead, their moss-covered trunks bearing witness to the passage of time. Bluebells blanket the forest floor in spring, creating a carpet of indigo that stretches as far as the eye can see. It is a place of enchantment, where the rhythms of nature unfold in a timeless dance.

In contrast to the ancient majesty of Silk Wood, the arboretum also features areas of more recent planting, showcasing a diverse array of tree species from around the world. The Downs, with its sweeping vistas and open grasslands, provides a canvas for the display of ornamental and exotic trees. Here, visitors can encounter the vibrant hues of maples, the graceful forms of conifers, and the delicate blossoms of flowering cherries. Each season brings its own palette of colors, from the fiery reds and oranges of autumn to the delicate pastels of spring.

One of the arboretum's most iconic attractions is the Tree Walk, a network of elevated walkways that allows visitors to explore the canopy of the trees. This unique perspective offers a bird's-eye view of the arboretum, revealing the intricate patterns of branches and foliage that make up this living tapestry. It is a chance to see the trees from a new angle, to appreciate the subtle details of their leaves and bark, and to experience the arboretum in a way that few have the opportunity to do.

For those seeking a more immersive experience, the arboretum offers a series of guided walks and educational programs led by knowledgeable arborists and naturalists. These programs delve into the ecological relationships between trees, wildlife, and the broader ecosystem. They also provide insights into the conservation efforts that are underway to safeguard the diversity of tree species for future generations.

Throughout the year, the arboretum hosts a calendar of events and activities that celebrate the beauty and significance of trees. From seasonal festivals that highlight the changing colors of the foliage to workshops on tree identification and propagation, there is always something to engage and inspire visitors of all ages.

The Westonbirt Arboretum is not only a place of botanical significance but also a refuge for wildlife. The diverse range of tree species provides habitats for a wide array of bird species, insects, and mammals. From the melodious song of warblers to the rustling of squirrels in the canopy, the arboretum is alive with the sights and sounds of nature.

In addition to its ecological importance, the arboretum serves as a living laboratory for research and conservation efforts. Horticulturists and scientists collaborate to study the growth patterns, genetic diversity, and adaptability of tree species, contributing to our understanding of how to safeguard these vital components of our natural heritage.

As the seasons paint their colors across the landscape, the Westonbirt Arboretum undergoes a transformation that is nothing short of magical. In spring, the woodlands burst forth in a riot of blossoms, and the air is alive with the hum of pollinators. Summer brings the heady scent of blooming flowers and the vibrant hues of butterfly wings. Autumn casts its golden spell, as the leaves of deciduous trees turn to shades of amber and russet, creating a scene of breathtaking beauty.

In winter, the landscape takes on a quiet elegance, with frost-kissed branches and the sculptural silhouettes of bare trees etched against the winter sky. The arboretum's timeless beauty knows no season, and each time of year brings its own unique enchantment.

For visitors, the Westonbirt Arboretum offers not only a place of botanical discovery but also a sanctuary for the soul. It is a place where the wonders of the natural world are on full display, where the senses are awakened, and where the beauty of trees is celebrated in all its diversity. It is a living testament to the enduring connection between humanity and the natural world, a reminder of the vital role that trees play in sustaining life on our planet. The Westonbirt Arboretum is not merely a collection of trees; it is a living legacy of biodiversity, a testament to the power of nature to inspire, educate, and enrich our lives.

3.12 Birdland Park and Gardens (Bourton-on-the-Water):

Nestled in the charming village of Bourton-on-the-Water, within the heart of the Cotswolds, lies a haven for avian enthusiasts and nature lovers alike—a place known as Birdland Park and Gardens. This unique sanctuary offers a captivating journey into the world of birds, where visitors can immerse themselves in the diverse and fascinating lives of avian species from around the globe. With its meticulously curated exhibits, lush gardens, and educational programs, Birdland provides an opportunity to appreciate the beauty, intelligence, and ecological importance of our feathered friends.

The origins of Birdland trace back to the mid-20th century when it was established by an avid bird enthusiast. Over the years, the park has grown and evolved, becoming a beloved destination for families, birdwatchers, and wildlife enthusiasts. Today, Birdland stands as a testament to the enduring fascination that birds hold for people of all ages.

The park is home to a diverse array of bird species, representing various habitats and continents. From the vibrant plumage of tropical parrots to the majestic presence of birds of prey, each exhibit offers a glimpse into the specialized adaptations and behaviors that make these creatures so captivating.

One of the highlights of Birdland is the Flamingo Lagoon, where a colony of vibrant pink flamingos wade and forage in the shallow waters. These graceful birds, with their distinctive curved beaks and long necks, evoke a sense of wonder and admiration. Visitors can observe their social interactions, their distinctive feeding behavior, and the synchronized movements that are characteristic of flamingo colonies.

The Penguin Shore, with its chilled pools and rocky terrain, provides a habitat for a colony of charismatic penguins. These endearing birds, known for their comical waddling gait and distinctive black and white plumage, are a favorite among visitors. They exhibit a range of behaviors, from swimming with remarkable agility to engaging in vocalizations that reflect their social dynamics.

The Marshmouth Nature Reserve, situated within the park, offers a tranquil haven for native British bird species and other wildlife. This wetland habitat, with its reed beds and waterways, provides a vital refuge for migratory birds and supports a rich diversity of life. It is a testament to the importance of preserving natural habitats for the well-being of both wildlife and the broader ecosystem.

One of the most captivating features of Birdland is the Discovery Zone, an interactive area that provides visitors with hands-on learning experiences. Here, educational programs and encounters with birds offer insights into their behavior, biology, and conservation. Visitors have the opportunity to meet and learn about birds up close, fostering a deeper appreciation for these remarkable creatures.

The Jurassic Journey, a prehistoric-themed exhibit, takes visitors on a journey back in time to the era of dinosaurs.

Here, life-sized models of ancient reptiles and birds provide a glimpse into the evolutionary history of avian species. It is a chance to explore the connections between birds and their ancient ancestors, offering a perspective on the enduring legacy of avian evolution.

In addition to its diverse collection of bird species, Birdland is home to a lush array of gardens and natural habitats. The River Windrush, which meanders through the park, adds a tranquil and scenic element to the landscape. The gardens, with their vibrant blooms and carefully curated plantings, create a harmonious environment that complements the avian inhabitants.

As the seasons unfold, the gardens undergo a transformation, painting the landscape with a kaleidoscope of colors. From the vibrant hues of spring blossoms to the rich tapestry of autumn foliage, each season brings its own unique beauty to the park. The sensory experience of the gardens, from the scent of blooming flowers to the rustling leaves, adds an extra dimension to the visit.

Birdland also plays a role in conservation efforts aimed at safeguarding bird species and their habitats. Through educational programs, research initiatives, and partnerships with conservation organizations, the park contributes to the broader mission of preserving biodiversity and raising awareness about the challenges facing bird populations worldwide.

For visitors, Birdland offers not only an opportunity to connect with the natural world but also a chance to be inspired by the beauty and diversity of birds. It is a place where the wonder of avian life comes to life, where the curiosity of children and the fascination of adults are kindled by the vibrant personalities and behaviors of these creatures.

It is a sanctuary for reflection, a place to appreciate the intricate interplay between birds and their environments, and a reminder of the importance of conservation efforts to ensure the survival of these remarkable species. Birdland Park and Gardens is more than a park; it is an invitation to explore, learn, and be inspired by the world of birds—a world that captivates the imagination and enriches our understanding of the natural world.

3.13 The Gloucestershire Warwickshire Steam Railway:

Nestled in the heart of the Cotswolds, the Gloucestershire Warwickshire Steam Railway offers a nostalgic voyage through time, where the golden age of steam locomotion comes to life. This heritage railway, lovingly restored and operated by dedicated volunteers, provides a unique opportunity to experience the magic of steam travel against the backdrop of the picturesque Cotswold countryside.

The history of the Gloucestershire Warwickshire Steam Railway dates back to the mid-19th century, when it was originally part of a network of railway lines that connected communities across the region. Over the years, economic shifts and changes in transportation led to the closure of many of these lines, including the section that now forms the heritage railway.

In the latter half of the 20th century, a group of passionate railway enthusiasts and preservationists came together with a shared vision: to breathe new life into this historic railway and share the experience of steam travel with future generations. Their dedication and tireless efforts culminated in the restoration and reopening of the Gloucestershire Warwickshire Steam Railway, which stands today as a living testament to their vision and commitment.

The heart of the railway lies in its meticulously restored steam locomotives and vintage carriages, each a masterpiece of engineering and craftsmanship. These lovingly maintained locomotives, many of which have been rescued and painstakingly restored, are living relics of a bygone era. As they come to life with billowing clouds of steam and the rhythmic chug of pistons, they evoke a sense of wonder and awe.

One of the key attractions of the Gloucestershire Warwickshire Steam Railway is the opportunity for visitors to step aboard these historic trains and embark on a journey through time. The leisurely pace of the steam train journey allows passengers to savor the scenic beauty of the Cotswolds, from rolling hills and meadows to quaint villages and historic landmarks. It is a chance to experience travel as it once was, a leisurely voyage that invites contemplation and connection with the landscape.

The railway offers a range of experiences, from short journeys between picturesque stations to themed events and dining experiences. Visitors can choose to ride in vintage carriages, each lovingly restored to reflect the elegance and charm of a bygone era. The attention to detail, from the polished brass and gleaming woodwork to the plush upholstery, creates an immersive experience that transports passengers to a different time.

The stations along the Gloucestershire Warwickshire Steam Railway are more than mere stops along the route; they are living museums that provide a window into the history of railway travel. The carefully preserved stations, with their period architecture and authentic signage, evoke the ambiance of a bustling railway hub from days gone by. Visitors can explore the platforms, visit the station buildings, and even catch a glimpse of the dedicated volunteers who keep the railway running.

One of the highlights of the railway is the Winchcombe Station, which serves as the headquarters and main terminus. This charming station, with its distinctive red-brick buildings and flower-filled gardens, exudes a timeless charm. It is here that visitors can learn about the history of the railway, explore the beautifully restored station buildings, and even enjoy a leisurely meal in the station's tearoom.

The Gloucestershire Warwickshire Steam Railway is more than a transportation experience; it is a journey through living history. Along the route, visitors may encounter reenactors and volunteers in period attire, adding an extra layer of authenticity to the experience. From stationmasters in traditional uniforms to railway workers tending to the locomotives, these dedicated individuals help bring the past to life.

The railway also hosts a variety of themed events throughout the year, ranging from vintage weekends to special seasonal celebrations. These events provide an opportunity for visitors to immerse themselves in the nostalgia of days gone by, with activities, displays, and entertainment that capture the spirit of the era.

In addition to its role as a living museum, the Gloucestershire Warwickshire Steam Railway plays a vital role in preserving and promoting the heritage of steam travel. The dedicated volunteers who operate and maintain the railway are the lifeblood of this endeavor, sharing their passion and expertise with visitors from around the world. Their commitment to excellence in restoration, operation, and safety ensures that the magic of steam travel continues to captivate audiences of all ages.

As the seasons unfold, the Gloucestershire Warwickshire Steam Railway undergoes a transformation that is nothing short of magical. In spring, the countryside comes alive with the vibrant hues of blossoming flowers and the fresh greenery of new growth. Summer brings the golden glow of sunshine, casting a warm light on the meadows and fields. Autumn paints the landscape in a tapestry of rich, earthy tones, as the leaves of deciduous trees turn to shades of amber and russet.

In winter, a quiet beauty blankets the countryside, with frost-kissed fields and bare branches etched against the winter sky. The steam from the locomotives mingles with the crisp air, creating an ethereal atmosphere. The Gloucestershire Warwickshire Steam Railway's timeless beauty knows no season, and each time of year brings its own unique enchantment.

For visitors, the Gloucestershire Warwickshire Steam Railway offers not only a chance to step back in time but also a connection to a heritage that continues to inspire and captivate. It is a place where the spirit of steam travel lives on, where the magic of locomotion and the beauty of the Cotswolds converge. It is an opportunity to share in the passion and dedication of the volunteers who keep this living museum alive—a testament to the enduring allure of steam locomotion in the heart of the Cotswolds.

3.14 Cotswold Pottery (Bourton-on-the-Water):

Nestled in the picturesque village of Bourton-on-the-Water, Cotswold Pottery stands as a testament to the enduring art of pottery-making. With its roots firmly planted in the heart of the Cotswolds, this artisanal pottery studio has become a beacon for those seeking handcrafted ceramics that marry artistry with functionality. Visitors to Cotswold Pottery are invited on a journey into the world of clay, where skilled potters shape and mold raw materials into exquisite pieces that capture the essence of the Cotswold landscape.

The story of Cotswold Pottery is one of passion, dedication, and a deep appreciation for the natural beauty of the region. Founded by a group of artisans who shared a love for pottery-making, the studio has been a hub for creativity and craftsmanship for decades. The potters at Cotswold Pottery draw inspiration from the rich tapestry of the Cotswolds, where rolling hills, meandering rivers, and quaint villages provide an endless source of creative fuel.

The pottery's signature style is a fusion of traditional techniques and contemporary design sensibilities. Each piece is a labor of love, from the careful selection of clay to the meticulous process of shaping, glazing, and firing. The result is a collection of ceramics that bear the distinctive touch of handcrafted artistry, where no two pieces are exactly alike.

Visitors to Cotswold Pottery have the opportunity to step into the world of the potter, where the sights, sounds, and textures of the craft come to life. The studio's open layout allows for an immersive experience, where visitors can witness the skilled hands of potters at work. From throwing on the wheel to hand-building intricate forms, every stage of the pottery-making process is on display.

For those seeking a hands-on experience, Cotswold Pottery offers workshops and classes that invite participants to try their hand at pottery-making. Under the guidance of experienced potters, attendees can unleash their creativity and craft their own ceramic creations. It's a chance to feel the clay between their fingers, to shape and mold it into forms that reflect their own unique vision.

The showroom at Cotswold Pottery is a treasure trove of ceramic delights, showcasing a diverse range of pieces created by the studio's talented artisans. From functional tableware to decorative sculptures, the collection spans a spectrum of styles and forms. Visitors can explore the shelves, admiring the craftsmanship and artistry that infuses each piece with character and charm.

One of the hallmarks of Cotswold Pottery is its commitment to sustainable and locally sourced materials. The clay used in the studio's creations is sourced from nearby quarries, ensuring a connection to the land from which it originates. This commitment to sustainability extends to the studio's firing process, where energy-efficient kilns are employed to reduce environmental impact.

The ceramics created at Cotswold Pottery are more than mere objects; they are vessels that carry the spirit of the Cotswolds. Each piece reflects the natural beauty and timeless charm of the region, whether through earthy, rustic glazes that evoke the hues of the landscape or delicate, botanical motifs inspired by the flora of the Cotswold meadows.

The studio's location in Bourton-on-the-Water adds an extra layer of inspiration to the creative process. The village, with its quaint stone bridges and meandering River Windrush, provides a picturesque backdrop that finds its way into the pottery's designs. Visitors can see echoes of the village's charm in the forms and patterns of the ceramics, creating a tangible link between the art and its surroundings.

Cotswold Pottery's commitment to community and craftsmanship extends beyond its studio walls. The pottery hosts events, exhibitions, and collaborations with local artists, fostering a sense of camaraderie and creative exchange. It serves as a hub for artists and enthusiasts to come together, sharing their love for ceramics and the Cotswolds.

As the seasons change, so too does the inspiration for the pottery creations. Spring may bring forth delicate floral motifs and pastel hues, while autumn might be reflected in the warm, earthy tones of glazes. The ceramics of Cotswold Pottery are a living canvas that evolves with the rhythm of the natural world, providing a reflection of the cyclical beauty of the Cotswold landscape.

For visitors, Cotswold Pottery offers not only a chance to admire and acquire exquisite ceramics but also an opportunity to connect with the artisans who bring them to life. It is a place where the art of pottery-making is celebrated and shared, where the creative spirit finds its expression in the tactile beauty of clay. Cotswold Pottery is a testament to the enduring appeal of handmade craftsmanship and the profound connection between art, nature, and community.

CHAPTER FOUR

NAVIGATING COTSWOLDS

4.1 Transportation Options

When embarking on a journey through the Cotswolds, one of England's most captivating regions, travelers have the privilege of choosing from a variety of transportation options tailored to their preferences and travel needs. Each mode of transportation offers a unique perspective and a distinct set of advantages, ensuring that every traveler can navigate this picturesque area in a way that suits them best.

Car Rental: The Freedom of Independent Exploration

Renting a car in the Cotswolds is akin to unlocking a realm of boundless exploration. It grants you the freedom to chart your own course, discover hidden gems, and set your own pace. The convenience of having your own vehicle allows for spontaneous detours, ensuring that no charming village or scenic overlook goes unexplored. However, before you hit the road, take a moment to familiarize yourself with local driving laws and road conditions. The Cotswolds' narrow, winding lanes and occasional wildlife crossings call for a cautious and considerate approach. Armed with this knowledge, a rented car becomes your ticket to a truly personalized Cotswold adventure.

Public Transportation: Navigating with Ease and Efficiency

For those who prefer to leave the driving to others, the Cotswolds boasts a well-connected public transportation network that seamlessly links its charming towns and villages. Buses and trains crisscross the countryside, offering a reliable and efficient means of getting from one enchanting locale to the next. Timetables and route information can be readily obtained from visitor centers or through online resources. This accessible network ensures that even without a personal vehicle, the treasures of the Cotswolds remain easily within reach, providing a stress-free travel experience for those who prefer to let someone else do the navigating.

Guided Tours: Curated Adventures with Expert Insight

For travelers seeking a curated and immersive Cotswold experience, guided tours offer an enticing option. These expert-led excursions provide not only transportation but also the invaluable knowledge and insight of seasoned guides. They breathe life into the history, culture, and natural beauty of the Cotswolds, enriching your journey with stories and facts that might otherwise remain undiscovered. Guided tours are thoughtfully designed, often incorporating carefully selected itineraries that showcase the very best of the region. This hassle-free approach allows you to simply relax and absorb the scenery, secure in the knowledge that every aspect of your adventure has been expertly arranged.

Opting for a guided tour in the Cotswolds means surrendering the stress of planning and navigation, leaving you free to savor the moment and revel in the splendor of your surroundings. It's an opportunity to glean a deeper understanding of the Cotswolds' rich heritage and to forge connections with fellow travelers under the guidance of a knowledgeable leader.

In conclusion, the transportation options in the Cotswolds are as diverse as the landscapes themselves. Whether you're enticed by the prospect of independent exploration with a rental car, drawn to the convenience of public transportation, or intrigued by the insights offered by guided tours, the Cotswolds invites you to discover its wonders on your own terms. With each option offering its own unique blend of freedom, convenience, and expertise, your Cotswold journey is poised to become an unforgettable adventure, tailored precisely to your travel inclinations.

4.2 Getting Around Cities

In the enchanting Cotswolds, each city and town is a treasure trove of unique charm and captivating attractions. To truly savor the essence of these places, it's essential to navigate them in a way that allows you to soak in their distinctive character. Here are some insightful tips on getting around in this picturesque region:

Walking: A Stroll Through Timeless Beauty

Many of the Cotswolds' towns are blessed with a compact layout and a pedestrian-friendly environment. This makes walking one of the most pleasurable and immersive ways to explore the local wonders. Meander down cobbled streets lined with honey-hued cottages, wander into boutique shops brimming with handmade crafts, and pause at historic sites that whisper tales of centuries gone by. With each step, you'll uncover the hidden nooks and crannies that make each Cotswold town a true gem.

Bicycles: Embracing Scenic Journeys

For those eager to cover more ground while reveling in the breathtaking countryside, bicycles provide an idyllic mode of transportation. Some Cotswold towns offer bicycle rentals, presenting an opportunity to embark on leisurely rides through rolling hills and verdant valleys. With the wind in your hair and the scent of wildflowers in the air, you'll forge a deeper connection with the natural beauty that defines this region.

Local Transport: Efficient Urban Exploration

In larger towns and cities across the Cotswolds, a network of public buses and trams ensures efficient navigation within urban areas. This mode of transport proves especially valuable when you're looking to explore a wider range of attractions within a concentrated space. Hop on a bus or tram, and you'll effortlessly move from historic landmarks to vibrant marketplaces, all while enjoying the convenience of reliable and punctual urban transit.

By embracing these diverse modes of transportation, you'll not only move from one point to another but also immerse yourself in the heart of the Cotswolds. Whether it's the intimate exploration of charming streets on foot, the liberating rides through the countryside on a bicycle, or the efficient urban journeys via local transport, each mode offers a unique perspective on this captivating region.

In the Cotswolds, getting around isn't just about reaching your destination; it's an integral part of the experience itself. It's about discovering the intricate details that define each town and city, and about forging a connection with the land and its heritage. So, as you navigate the Cotswolds, let each step, pedal, or ride be a gateway to a deeper appreciation of this timeless corner of England.

4.3 Travel Safety Tips

Ensuring your safety during your Cotswolds adventure is paramount. The idyllic landscapes and historic sites should be explored with confidence and peace of mind. Here are some essential travel safety tips to keep in mind:

- Stay Informed: Familiarize yourself with local emergency numbers and the nearest medical facilities. Having this information readily available can make a crucial difference in case of any unforeseen events. It's also wise to stay updated on weather forecasts, especially if you plan on engaging in outdoor activities.
- Weather Preparedness: The weather in the Cotswolds can be unpredictable, with sudden shifts from sunshine to rain. Pack layers and waterproof gear to stay comfortable. If embarking on hikes or long walks, ensure you have appropriate footwear and, if needed, a walking stick for added stability on uneven terrain.
- Personal Belongings: Keep valuables secure and be aware of your surroundings, especially in crowded areas. A crossbody bag with a secure closure can be a practical choice. Avoid carrying large sums of cash and opt for card payments when possible. Consider

using a money belt or hidden pouch for added security.

- Health Precautions: Prioritize your well-being by packing any necessary medications and a basic first aid kit. If you have specific dietary requirements or allergies, communicate these clearly when dining out. It's also advisable to carry a refillable water bottle to stay hydrated, especially during outdoor activities.
- Transportation Safety: Whether driving or using public transport, observe local traffic rules and exercise caution on narrow, winding roads. Ensure that you're adequately insured if renting a car. When using public transportation, be mindful of schedules and routes to avoid unnecessary delays or confusion.
- Local Etiquette: Respecting local customs and etiquette is key to a positive travel experience. For example, it's customary to greet people with a polite "good morning" or "good afternoon." When visiting churches or other religious sites, modest attire is appreciated.

By adhering to these travel safety tips, you'll not only safeguard your well-being but also enhance your overall enjoyment of the Cotswolds. Exploring this enchanting region becomes a true delight when you can do so with confidence and ease, knowing that you're well-prepared for any situation that may arise.

4.4 Tips for Navigating Public Transportation

Using public transportation in the Cotswolds can be a convenient and eco-friendly way to explore the region. Here are some valuable tips to ensure a smooth and efficient experience:

- Timetables and Routes: Familiarize yourself with local transportation schedules and routes. This knowledge is invaluable for planning your journeys. Timetables can typically be accessed online through official transportation websites or mobile apps. Additionally, physical copies may be available at transportation hubs, visitor centers, or even local shops. Understanding the schedules ensures you won't miss out on any must-see destinations or experiences.

- Payment Methods: Understand the payment options for public transportation, which may include cash, contactless cards, or mobile apps. Different methods of payment are often available, and it's beneficial to know which one best suits your needs. Some transportation systems accept cash, while others rely on contactless payment cards or mobile apps. Having the appropriate payment method on hand streamlines your travel and minimizes any potential delays.

- Tickets and Passes: Consider purchasing day passes or multi-ride tickets, which can offer cost savings for frequent travelers. If you plan on using public transportation frequently during your Cotswolds adventure, investing in day passes or multi-ride tickets can be a cost-effective choice. These options often provide substantial savings compared to purchasing individual tickets for each leg of your journey. They also grant you the freedom to hop on and off various modes of transportation without the hassle of purchasing a new ticket every time.

By keeping these tips in mind, you'll be well-prepared to make the most of the Cotswolds' public transportation system. Whether you're exploring charming villages or venturing into urban centers, a well-informed approach ensures your travels are both efficient and enjoyable. This eco-conscious mode of exploration allows you to fully appreciate the natural beauty and cultural richness of the region, all while minimizing your environmental impact.

4.5 Travel Insurance and Health Precautions

Embarking on a journey, especially to a region as rich and diverse as the Cotswolds, demands careful preparation. Travelers must prioritize their well-being to fully savor the experience. This involves a twofold approach: securing the appropriate insurance coverage and taking necessary health precautions.

Travel Insurance: Your Safety Net

Travel insurance acts as a safety net, providing a buffer against unforeseen circumstances that could disrupt your journey. It encompasses a range of protections, from trip cancellations to medical emergencies. For a Cotswolds adventure, comprehensive travel insurance should be a non-negotiable part of your travel plan.

Picture a scenario where unexpected events force you to cancel or truncate your trip. Travel insurance steps in, covering non-refundable expenses and alleviating financial strain. Additionally, in the event of a medical emergency, having insurance ensures you receive necessary care without incurring exorbitant out-of-pocket costs. This encompasses everything from hospital stays to emergency evacuations, expenses that can quickly escalate without proper coverage.

Health Precautions: Prioritizing Your Well-being

In addition to insurance, it's crucial to take health precautions to maintain your well-being during your Cotswolds adventure. This includes packing any necessary medications and a basic first aid kit. Communicate dietary requirements or allergies clearly when dining out, ensuring that your culinary experiences are both enjoyable and safe. Moreover, carrying a refillable water bottle is highly advisable to stay hydrated, particularly during outdoor activities.

By taking these measures, you're not only safeguarding your health but also enhancing your overall travel experience. It's a proactive approach that allows you to revel in the Cotswolds' beauty and heritage without unnecessary worry. With the right coverage and health precautions, your journey becomes an enriching and unforgettable exploration of this timeless corner of England.

4.5.1 The Importance of Travel Insurance

Travel insurance is your safety net, providing financial protection and peace of mind in the face of unexpected events. It acts as a guardian against a range of potential mishaps, from trip cancellations to medical emergencies. For your Cotswolds expedition, securing comprehensive travel insurance should be a priority.

Imagine unforeseen circumstances forcing you to cancel or cut short your trip. Travel insurance can cover non-refundable expenses, allowing you to recoup losses. Moreover, in the event of a medical emergency, having travel insurance ensures that you receive necessary care without incurring exorbitant out-of-pocket costs. From hospital stays to emergency evacuations, these expenses can be substantial, making insurance a vital component of your travel plan.

Types of Coverage to Consider

- Trip Cancellation/Interruption: This coverage safeguards your financial investment in the trip. It reimburses non-refundable expenses if your journey is cancelled or unexpectedly curtailed due to covered reasons, such as illness, injury, or unforeseen events.
- Medical Coverage: Health emergencies can happen anywhere, and being prepared is crucial. Medical coverage ensures you're protected in case of illness or injury during your Cotswolds adventure. This includes doctor visits, hospital stays, prescription medications, and even emergency medical evacuation if needed.
- Baggage Loss/Delay: While the Cotswolds may enchant you, the possibility of luggage mishaps remains. This coverage provides compensation for lost, stolen, or delayed luggage, ensuring you can replace essentials and continue your journey without undue stress.
- Travel Assistance: Navigating unfamiliar territory can be daunting, especially in the event of a crisis. Travel assistance services offer invaluable support, from medical referrals to translation services. This invaluable resource can help you navigate any unexpected challenges with confidence.

As you explore the Cotswolds' captivating landscapes and historic sites, having the right insurance coverage in place ensures that you can fully immerse yourself in the experience without worry. It's a safeguard that allows you to cherish each moment, secure in the knowledge that you're prepared for any unforeseen circumstances.

CHAPTER FIVE

ACCOMMODATION

5.1 Hotels and Resorts

The Cotswolds, a region steeped in natural beauty and timeless charm, offers an array of exquisite hotels and resorts that harmonize with the picturesque surroundings. These accommodations range from opulent country estates to luxurious boutique hotels, each promising an immersive experience that mirrors the Cotswolds' distinctive character.

For those seeking a taste of grandeur, the Cotswolds proudly presents elegant country estates. These regal abodes, often nestled amidst sprawling manicured gardens, exude a sense of historic opulence. Guests are transported back in time, enveloped in luxurious furnishings and fine architectural details. The ambience is one of refined indulgence, with impeccable service complementing the grandeur.

In contrast, the region also boasts an impressive selection of boutique hotels, where contemporary flair meets the Cotswolds' timeless allure. These intimate retreats offer a personalized touch, with individually designed rooms showcasing a blend of modern comforts and local aesthetics. The emphasis here is on curated experiences, ensuring guests feel a profound connection to both their lodgings and the surrounding landscape.

What truly distinguishes Cotswold accommodations is their symbiotic relationship with nature. Many establishments afford breathtaking views of the rolling hills, seamlessly integrating the outdoors into the guest experience. Spa facilities, often perched amidst serene surroundings, beckon visitors to rejuvenate in the lap of nature. Likewise, fine dining restaurants celebrate the region's bounty, offering culinary experiences that pay homage to local, seasonal produce.

Furthermore, these accommodations serve as gateways to a wealth of activities and experiences. Guided walks through ancient woodlands, visits to charming villages, and leisurely picnics along the riverbanks are just a taste of what awaits guests. With each stay, visitors become not merely spectators, but active participants in the Cotswolds' timeless narrative.

Recommended Hotels And Resorts With Their Locations

The Lygon Arms

Location: High Street, Broadway, Worcestershire WR12 7DU

Description: Situated in the heart of Broadway, The Lygon Arms is a historic hotel dating back to the 16th century. It offers a perfect blend of period charm, modern amenities, and impeccable service.

Calcot & Spa

Location: Tetbury, Gloucestershire GL8 8YJ

Description: Nestled in a secluded valley, Calcot & Spa is a luxurious retreat offering elegant rooms, a spa, and an award-winning restaurant. It's surrounded by picturesque countryside.

Ellenborough Park

Location: Southam Road, Cheltenham, Gloucestershire GL52 3NJ

Description: Set within a magnificent 15th-century manor, Ellenborough Park combines historic grandeur with contemporary comfort. The hotel overlooks Cheltenham Racecourse.

Dormy House Hotel and Spa

Location: Willersey Hill, Broadway, Worcestershire WR12 7LF

Description: This stylish boutique hotel in Broadway offers chic and comfortable rooms, a top-notch spa, and a variety of dining options. It's nestled in the picturesque Cotswold countryside.

The Greenway Hotel & Spa

Location: Shurdington Road, Cheltenham, Gloucestershire GL51 4UG

Description: A charming country house hotel near Cheltenham, The Greenway offers elegant rooms, a spa, and a fine dining restaurant. It's surrounded by lush gardens.

Barnsley House

Location: Barnsley, Cirencester, Gloucestershire GL7 5EE

Description: A quintessential English country house hotel, Barnsley House boasts beautifully designed rooms, a tranquil garden, and an excellent restaurant.

Lower Slaughter Manor

Location: Lower Slaughter, Cheltenham, Gloucestershire GL54 2HP

Description: This stunning manor house hotel in Lower Slaughter exudes luxury and charm. It features elegant rooms, exquisite dining, and a serene setting along the River Eye.

5.2 Boutique Stays

In the heart of the Cotswolds, boutique stays offer a uniquely intimate and personalized experience, making them a cherished choice for discerning travelers. These enchanting accommodations, often nestled within centuries-old buildings, exude character and charm, immersing guests in the authentic essence of the region.

Boutique stays in the Cotswolds are a celebration of individuality. Each establishment boasts its own distinctive style, carefully curated to reflect the heritage and aesthetics of its surroundings. From quaint inns adorned with original beams to stylish bed-and-breakfasts tucked away in picturesque villages, these lodgings are a testament to the owners' dedication to creating an atmosphere of warmth and comfort.

One of the defining features of boutique stays is the exceptional level of service. With fewer rooms to attend to, hosts can provide personalized attention to every guest. This fosters a sense of familiarity and a genuine connection between hosts and visitors, creating an atmosphere akin to staying with dear friends.

In these smaller, independently-run establishments, attention to detail is paramount. Rooms are often individually designed, showcasing a blend of vintage charm and modern amenities. Guests can expect unique furnishings, cozy linens, and thoughtful touches that make for a truly memorable stay.

Perhaps one of the most enchanting aspects of boutique stays in the Cotswolds is their integration into the local community. Many are situated in the heart of villages, allowing guests to immerse themselves in the day-to-day life of the region. This proximity provides easy access to quaint shops, inviting pubs, and the inviting hum of village life.

For travelers seeking an experience that transcends the ordinary, boutique stays in the Cotswolds offer a world of enchantment. Here, amidst the timeless beauty of the English countryside, every moment is imbued with a sense of grace and authenticity, promising a stay that lingers in the memory long after the journey has ended.

Recommended Boutique Stays With Their Locations

The Wheatsheaf Inn

Location: West End, Northleach, Cheltenham, Gloucestershire GL54 3EZ

Description: Nestled in the heart of the Cotswolds, The Wheatsheaf Inn offers cozy and individually designed rooms, a welcoming pub atmosphere, and a focus on locally sourced cuisine.

The Painswick

Location: Kemps Lane, Painswick, Stroud, Gloucestershire GL6 6YB

Description: Set in the charming village of Painswick, The Painswick is a stylish boutique hotel featuring beautifully appointed rooms, a garden terrace, and stunning views of the Cotswold countryside.

The Wild Rabbit

Location: Church Street, Kingham, Chipping Norton, Oxfordshire OX7 6YA

Description: This idyllic inn in the village of Kingham offers rustic-chic rooms, a focus on sustainability, and a renowned restaurant showcasing locally sourced, seasonal ingredients.

No. 131

Location: The Promenade, Cheltenham, Gloucestershire GL50 1NW

Description: Located in the heart of Cheltenham, No. 131 is a stylish boutique hotel with individually designed rooms, a vibrant bar, and a restaurant known for its creative cuisine.

The Lamb Inn

Location: Sheep Street, Burford, Oxfordshire OX18 4LR

Description: A historic inn in the charming town of Burford, The Lamb Inn offers characterful rooms, a traditional pub setting, and a restaurant featuring locally sourced produce.

The Swan Inn

Location: Bibury, Cirencester, Gloucestershire GL7 5NW

Description: Situated in the iconic village of Bibury, The Swan Inn provides boutique rooms with a blend of modern comfort and historic charm. It also boasts a delightful garden and a cozy pub.

The Ebrington Arms

Location: Ebrington, Chipping Campden, Gloucestershire GL55 6NH

Description: Tucked away in the village of Ebrington, The Ebrington Arms is a quintessential English pub with boutique rooms, a warm and welcoming atmosphere, and a focus on local ales and cuisine.

5.3 Budget-Friendly Options

For budget-conscious travelers, the Cotswolds offer a welcoming array of accommodation options that provide comfort without straining the wallet. These wallet-friendly choices allow visitors to experience the enchantment of the Cotswolds without compromising on quality.

Cozy guesthouses and family-run inns dot the landscape, providing a warm and inviting atmosphere. These establishments often exude a home-away-from-home vibe, with attentive hosts who are eager to share their local knowledge. Guests can expect clean, comfortable rooms and a hearty breakfast to start their day of exploration.

Hostels are another popular choice for budget travelers. They provide a communal and sociable environment, making them ideal for solo travelers or those seeking to connect with like-minded adventurers. Cotswold hostels often boast modern amenities, clean facilities, and convenient locations near popular attractions.

Self-catering cottages and holiday apartments offer a cost-effective option for families or groups. These accommodations provide the freedom to prepare meals, allowing guests to save on dining expenses. They are often nestled within charming villages, providing an authentic Cotswolds experience.

Campgrounds and caravan parks cater to outdoor enthusiasts and those seeking a closer connection to nature. With basic facilities and stunning natural surroundings, these options offer a budget-friendly way to experience the Cotswolds' countryside.

Furthermore, some budget-friendly accommodations offer special deals and packages, especially during off-peak seasons. These promotions can provide even greater value for money, allowing guests to make the most of their visit.

It's worth noting that despite being budget-friendly, these accommodations do not compromise on the essence of the Cotswolds experience. Visitors will still find themselves immersed in the region's timeless beauty, surrounded by quaint villages, rolling hills, and a rich tapestry of history and culture.

Ultimately, the Cotswolds extend a warm welcome to travelers of all budgets, ensuring that everyone has the opportunity to savor the magic of this captivating English countryside.

Recommended Budget-Friendly Options With Their Locations

YHA Stow-on-the-Wold

Location: The Square, Stow-on-the-Wold, Gloucestershire GL54 1AF

Description: This budget-friendly hostel in Stow-on-the-Wold offers comfortable dormitory-style accommodation with shared facilities. It's a great option for travelers on a budget.

The George Inn

Location: High Street, Norton St Philip, Bath BA2 7LH

Description: Located in the village of Norton St Philip, The George Inn offers affordable rooms in a traditional pub setting. It's a convenient base for exploring the Cotswolds.

The Bell Inn

Location: High Street, Moreton-in-Marsh, Gloucestershire GL56 0AF

Description: Situated in the heart of Moreton-in-Marsh, The Bell Inn provides budget-friendly rooms in a historic coaching inn. It's a great option for those seeking value for money.

The Fox Inn

Location: Great Barrington, Burford, Oxfordshire OX18 4TB

Description: Nestled in the village of Great Barrington, The Fox Inn offers affordable rooms in a charming country pub. It provides a cozy and budget-friendly option for travelers.

The Wheatsheaf Inn

Location: Sheep Street, Banbury, Oxfordshire OX15 0PS

Description: Located in the market town of Banbury, The Wheatsheaf Inn offers budget-friendly accommodation in a traditional English pub setting. It's a comfortable choice for budget-conscious travelers.

The Unicorn Inn

Location: Stow Road, Stow-on-the-Wold, Gloucestershire GL54 1DU

Description: Situated on the outskirts of Stow-on-the-Wold, The Unicorn Inn offers affordable rooms in a charming village pub. It provides a relaxed and budget-friendly stay.

The Crown Inn

Location: High Street, Blockley, Moreton-in-Marsh, Gloucestershire GL56 9EX

Description: Located in the peaceful village of Blockley, The Crown Inn offers budget-friendly rooms in a historic coaching inn. It's a tranquil option for those seeking affordability.

5.4 Booking Accommodation in Advance

With the Cotswolds being a highly sought-after tourist destination, particularly during peak seasons, it is highly recommended to secure your accommodation well in advance. This strategic approach not only grants you access to a diverse array of options but also assures a seamless and stress-free travel experience. The Cotswolds' popularity as a destination for its picturesque villages, historic sites, and natural splendor means that accommodations can be in high demand, particularly in charming locales like Bibury, Broadway, and Stow-on-the-Wold.

By reserving your lodging early, you gain the advantage of choosing from a wide spectrum of establishments, ranging from cozy bed-and-breakfasts to elegant country estates. This way, you can tailor your stay to perfectly align with your travel preferences, whether you seek the quaint intimacy of a boutique stay or the full-service amenities of a luxury resort.

It's important to note that some of the most coveted properties in the Cotswolds tend to fill up quickly, especially during the summer and holiday seasons. Thus, proactively planning your accommodation ensures you secure your preferred choice, allowing you to fully immerse yourself in the region's captivating atmosphere without any last-minute uncertainties.

Furthermore, advanced booking affords you the opportunity to consider additional factors that may be of importance, such as room preferences, accessibility options, or any specific amenities you may require. By reserving early, you can communicate any special requests or accommodations you may need, guaranteeing a comfortable and tailored experience.

In essence, early accommodation booking in the Cotswolds not only offers peace of mind but also allows you to optimize your stay in this enchanting region. It provides you the freedom to select lodgings that resonate with your personal tastes and requirements, ensuring that your visit to the Cotswolds is a truly memorable one. So, whether you're seeking a picturesque countryside retreat or a charming village inn, securing your accommodation in advance is a strategic step towards a delightful and unforgettable Cotswolds adventure.

5.5 Tips for Finding the Right Lodging for Your Needs

- Consider Location: When choosing accommodation in the Cotswolds, decide whether you'd prefer the vibrant energy of a bustling town center or the serene tranquility of a countryside retreat. Each offers a distinct experience, allowing you to tailor your stay to your desired atmosphere.
- Amenities and Services: Identify the amenities that hold importance for you. Whether it's reliable Wi-Fi for staying connected, convenient parking, pet-friendly facilities, or indulgent spa services, knowing your priorities ensures a comfortable and enjoyable stay.
- Read Reviews: Take the time to peruse reviews from previous guests. Their experiences offer valuable insights into the quality of the accommodation and

the level of hospitality you can expect. This firsthand feedback can guide your decision-making process.

- Ask for Recommendations: Don't hesitate to tap into local knowledge or seek advice from travel forums. Locals and experienced travelers often hold valuable insights and may recommend hidden gems that might not be readily apparent in online listings.
- Check Cancellation Policies: It's essential to understand the cancellation policies of your chosen accommodation. Unforeseen circumstances may arise, and having a clear understanding of the cancellation terms can provide peace of mind and flexibility in case your plans need adjustment.
- Budget Considerations: Determine a budget range for your accommodation and stick to it. This not only helps manage your overall travel expenses but also streamlines your options. It ensures you find a place that not only meets your preferences but also aligns with your financial means, allowing you to fully enjoy your Cotswolds experience.

CHAPTER SIX

DINING IN COTSWOLDS

6.1 Cotswold Cuisine: Must Taste Dishes

The Cotswolds, known for their rich culinary heritage, offer a delectable array of dishes that are a must-try for any visitor. Here are some must-taste dishes in the Cotswolds:

- Cotswold Lamb: A Gastronomic Ode to Agriculture

Among the culinary treasures of the Cotswolds, none stand taller than the succulent Cotswold lamb. Raised on the lush pastures of the region, these lambs are a testament to the area's agricultural prowess. Expertly prepared with a symphony of fresh herbs and seasonings, every bite offers a taste of the land's rich bounty. The meat, tender and flavorful, embodies the essence of the Cotswolds' dedication to quality and tradition.

- Steak and Ale Pie: Comfort in Every Bite

For a taste of true British comfort food, look no further than the iconic Steak and Ale Pie. This beloved dish weaves a tale of tender beef cuts, slow-cooked to perfection, swimming in a rich ale-infused gravy. Encased in a flaky pastry crust, it is a marriage of hearty flavors and comforting textures, a dish that warms the soul with every delectable bite.

- Cream Tea: Timeless Elegance in Every Sip

Elevating teatime to an art form, the Cream Tea is a quintessential British delight not to be missed. Freshly baked scones, warm and buttery, are adorned with generous dollops of clotted cream and sweet, luscious jam. Paired with a pot of steaming, aromatic tea, this ritual is a celebration of time-honored elegance, an experience that invites you to savor every moment.

- Cotswold Cheese Platter: A Tapestry of Flavors

Embark on a delightful journey through the Cotswold cheese-making tradition with a carefully curated Cheese Platter. Featuring varieties such as Double Gloucester and the intriguingly named Stinking Bishop, each cheese is a testament to the region's artisanal craftsmanship. Paired with local chutneys and served alongside crusty bread, this tasting experience is a symphony of flavors that dance on the palate.

- Trout from the River Windrush: A Taste of Local Waters

Savor the fruits of the local waters with the Trout from the River Windrush, a delicacy that pays homage to the Cotswolds' natural bounty. Often prepared pan-fried, the trout is adorned with a medley of fresh herbs, creating a dish that encapsulates the pristine flavors of the river.

- Cider-Glazed Pork: A Sweet-Savory Symphony

Experience a harmonious blend of flavors with Cider-Glazed Pork, a dish that showcases the region's renowned apple cider. Locally-sourced pork, succulent and tender, is bathed in a glaze of this famous elixir, resulting in a marriage of sweet and savory notes that dance on the taste buds.

- Black Pudding: A Classic Reimagined

Embrace the rich, robust flavors of the Cotswolds with Black Pudding, a classic English blood sausage. Served with an array of accompaniments like apple sauce or poached eggs, this dish exemplifies the region's dedication to preserving culinary traditions.

- Sticky Toffee Pudding: A Sweet Symphony of Comfort

Indulge in the sumptuous embrace of Sticky Toffee Pudding, a dessert that promises to satisfy even the most discerning sweet tooth. A warm, moist sponge cake, bathed in a pool of rich toffee sauce, creates a symphony of textures and flavors that evoke a sense of comforting indulgence.

- Asparagus: A Springtime Delicacy

During the spring season, the Cotswolds unveil their renowned asparagus, celebrated for its delicate flavor and vibrant green hue. Served fresh and tender, it is a testament to the region's dedication to celebrating seasonal produce.

- Ploughman's Lunch: Rustic Simplicity at Its Best

Experience a traditional pub lunch with the Ploughman's Lunch, a rustic spread that speaks to the heart of Cotswold fare. A foundation of crusty, hearty bread provides the canvas for an array of sharp cheeses, tangy pickles, and a bed of fresh, crisp greens. It's a simple yet immensely satisfying culinary experience that embodies the essence of honest, wholesome eating.

- Beef and Ale Stew: Hearty Nourishment for the Soul

Warm your heart and soul with the comforting embrace of Beef and Ale Stew, a hearty dish that exemplifies the Cotswolds' commitment to warm, nourishing meals. Slow-cooked beef, tender and succulent, is lovingly simmered in a robust ale-based broth, then served with a medley of root vegetables. It's a dish that brings together the rustic flavors of the region in a bowl of heartwarming goodness.

- Eton Mess: A Medley of Textures and Flavors

Conclude your culinary journey with the delightful Eton Mess, a dessert that marries textures and flavors in perfect harmony. Crushed meringue, light and airy, mingles with fresh, juicy berries and a billowy cloud of whipped cream. It's a playful and indulgent medley that provides a sweet and satisfying conclusion to your Cotswold feast.

In every dish, the Cotswolds offer a taste of history, tradition, and a deep connection to the land. Each bite is an invitation to savor the essence of this captivating region, where culinary artistry thrives and flavors speak to the heart. As you explore the Cotswolds, allow your taste buds to be your guide, and let the rich tapestry of flavors paint a delicious portrait of this remarkable corner of England.

6.2 Farmers' Markets: Sampling Local Delights

One of the best ways to experience the authentic flavors of the Cotswolds is by visiting the vibrant farmers' markets scattered throughout the region. These markets offer a treasure trove of fresh produce, artisanal products, and local delicacies.

Must-Visit Farmers' Markets:

Stroud Farmers' Market: Where Organic Excellence Thrives

Nestled in the heart of the Cotswolds, Stroud Farmers' Market stands as a beacon of organic excellence. Here, local farmers proudly present their bountiful harvests, cultivated with care and a commitment to sustainable practices. Vibrant arrays of seasonal fruits and vegetables form a vivid tapestry, showcasing the rich diversity of the region's agriculture. In addition to the fresh produce, the market's stalls are adorned with an array of artisan crafts, from hand-spun textiles to intricately designed pottery, providing a glimpse into the skilled craftsmanship of the Cotswolds.

Cirencester Farmers' Market: A Bustling Cornucopia of Local Treasures

The market square in Cirencester transforms into a bustling cornucopia of local treasures during the farmers' market days. Here, the air is filled with the enticing aromas of freshly baked bread, artisanal cheeses, and an array of prepared foods that highlight the Cotswolds' culinary prowess. As you weave through the stalls, you'll find a diverse range of goods, from homemade jams and preserves to freshly cut flowers and plants. The vibrant atmosphere, coupled with the wide variety of offerings, creates an immersive experience that celebrates the vitality of the Cotswold community.

Moreton-in-Marsh Market: A Glimpse into Cotswold Life

Moreton-in-Marsh Market provides a captivating glimpse into the heart of Cotswold life. This market exudes a sense of bustling energy, drawing locals and visitors alike to explore its diverse offerings. Stroll along the cobbled streets and peruse the stalls, where a myriad of goods awaits discovery. From locally sourced meats and cheeses to artisanal crafts and antiques, the market encapsulates the essence of the Cotswolds – a blend of tradition, community, and a deep appreciation for quality craftsmanship.

Visiting these farmers' markets is not only an opportunity to sample the finest produce and products of the Cotswolds but also a chance to connect with the passionate individuals who dedicate themselves to preserving the region's culinary and artisanal heritage. It's a sensory journey, where the sights, sounds, and scents of the market become an integral part of your Cotswold experience. As you leave, laden with your chosen treasures, you carry with you a piece of the Cotswolds' vibrant spirit and a deeper understanding of the people who call this region home.6.3 Cotswold Distilleries: Spirits with a Sense of Place

The Cotswolds are gaining recognition for their boutique distilleries producing high-quality spirits. Take a tour and tasting to discover the craftsmanship behind these uniquely local libations.

Notable Distilleries:

Nestled in the idyllic village of Stourton, The Cotswolds Distillery stands as a beacon of artisanal excellence. Renowned for its meticulous approach to spirits, this distillery has gained acclaim for its exceptional gin and single malt whisky. Each bottle is a testament to the dedication of the master distillers, who craft every batch with precision and care. The gin, a harmonious blend of botanicals, captures the essence of the Cotswolds' botanical-rich landscapes. Meanwhile, the single malt whisky embodies the spirit of the region, matured in specially selected casks to achieve a depth of flavor that speaks of tradition and innovation.

Siblings Distillery (Cheltenham): Botanical Infusions, Handcrafted Brilliance

Nestled in the heart of Cheltenham, Siblings Distillery is a testament to the art of small-batch, handcrafted gin production. Here, a passion for botanicals infuses every aspect of the distilling process. The result is a collection of gins that capture the essence of the Cotswolds in every sip. From the carefully curated selection of herbs and botanicals to the precise distillation process, each bottle is a labor of love. The gins produced here are not just beverages; they are a sensory journey through the vibrant flora of the Cotswolds, a testament to the dedication of the distillers, and a celebration of the region's natural abundance.

6.3 Afternoon Tea in the Cotswolds: Tradition and Indulgence

In the heart of the Cotswolds, the tradition of afternoon tea takes on a special charm, offering a respite from the world amidst the region's idyllic backdrop. It's a ritual of refinement, an opportunity to unwind and savor exquisite treats in an atmosphere steeped in history and natural beauty. The table is set with care, and soon, an array of delights is presented.

A Symphony of Flavors: Finger Sandwiches, Scones, and Pastries

The afternoon tea experience in the Cotswolds unfolds with a symphony of flavors. Delicate finger sandwiches, filled with an assortment of savory fillings, showcase the artistry of the culinary artisans. The scones, warm and crumbly, arrive adorned with generous dollops of clotted cream and jewel-bright jam, inviting you to experience this quintessential British indulgence. Each bite is a harmony of textures and tastes, a testament to the dedication of those who craft these delicacies.

Charming Tea Rooms: Where Time Stands Still

In the Cotswolds, the setting is as important as the tea itself. At Badgers Hall Tearooms in Chipping Campden, guests are enveloped in a cozy and quaint ambiance. The charming tearoom exudes a warmth that makes you feel right at home, as if you've stepped into a cherished family gathering.

Meanwhile, The Old Bakery Tearoom in Bourton-on-the-Water is renowned for its delightful cream teas. Nestled in the heart of this picturesque village, the tearoom invites you to linger a little longer. Its ambiance, infused with the character of the village, creates an enchanting backdrop for your afternoon tea experience.

In both tearooms, the attention to detail is evident, from the dainty china to the attentive service. It's not merely a meal; it's a journey through tradition, a moment of respite, and a celebration of the Cotswolds' timeless allure. As you sip your tea and savor each bite, you become part of a legacy of elegance and refinement that defines the Cotswolds afternoon tea experience.

6.4 Dining Etiquette

Dining in the Cotswolds is not just a culinary experience; it's a cultural affair steeped in tradition and refinement. To fully immerse yourself in this rich tapestry of manners, consider these essential points of British dining etiquette:

1. Seating Etiquette: Waiting with Grace

Upon entering a restaurant or tearoom in the Cotswolds, it's customary to wait to be seated by a member of the staff. This shows respect for the establishment's seating arrangements and allows for a smooth flow of service. Whether it's a charming village pub or an elegant fine dining restaurant, this practice is a nod to the region's commitment to hospitality and courtesy.

2. The Art of Utensils: An Inside-Out Approach

As you embark on your culinary journey, pay attention to the arrangement of utensils on the table. The Cotswolds, like much of Britain, follows the traditional inside-out rule. Start with the utensils farthest from your plate and work your way in. This ensures a seamless progression through the courses, allowing you to savor each dish with the appropriate implement.

3. Tipping: A Gesture of Appreciation

In the Cotswolds, tipping is a customary way to show appreciation for good service. While it is not obligatory, it is considered polite and respectful to leave a small gratuity for the staff who have worked hard to make your dining experience memorable. Typically, a gratuity of 10-15% of the bill is a standard practice in the region.

By observing these time-honored practices, you not only enhance your dining experience but also pay homage to the cultural heritage of the Cotswolds. It's a way to connect with the traditions that have shaped this enchanting region, and to show your respect for the people who dedicate themselves to providing exceptional hospitality. So, as you embark on your culinary journey through the Cotswolds, remember to embrace these etiquette tips and let them add an extra layer of authenticity to your dining experience.

6.5 Recommended Restaurants with Their Locations

Here are some highly recommended dining establishments in the Cotswolds along with their locations:

The Wild Rabbit (Kingham)

Address: Church Street, Kingham, Chipping Norton, OX7 6YA

The Potting Shed (Crudwell)

Address: The Rectory, Crudwell, Malmesbury, SN16 9EP

The Painswick (Painswick)

Address: Kemps Ln, Painswick, Stroud, GL6 6YB

The Kingham Plough (Kingham)

Address: The Green, Kingham, Chipping Norton, OX7 6YD

The Wheatsheaf Inn (Northleach)

Address: West End, Northleach, Cheltenham, GL54 3EZ

Please note that reservations are recommended, especially during peak tourist seasons.

CHAPTER SEVEN

ENTERTAINMENT AND NIGHTLIFE

7.1 Theatres and Performance Arts

The Cotswolds region boasts a vibrant arts scene, with a range of theatres and performance venues offering a diverse array of entertainment options. From classic plays to cutting-edge performances, visitors can immerse themselves in the rich cultural offerings of the area. Notable venues include:

Everyman Theatre (Cheltenham):

Nestled in the heart of Cheltenham, the Everyman Theatre stands as a beacon of cultural enrichment in the Cotswolds. This distinguished venue has earned its reputation as one of the region's premier performing arts centers. It hosts a wide range of productions that span the spectrum of theatrical genres, ensuring there's something for everyone to enjoy. From riveting dramas that tug at the heartstrings to uproarious comedies that leave audiences in stitches, the Everyman Theatre curates a diverse repertoire that reflects the dynamic nature of the performing arts.

Moreover, musical enthusiasts will find their cravings satisfied here, as the theater showcases an array of musicals, from timeless classics to cutting-edge contemporary productions. Dance aficionados are also in for a treat, with performances that range from classical ballet to avant-garde contemporary dance. The Everyman Theatre's commitment to offering a multifaceted cultural experience is a testament to its dedication to the arts and its role in enriching the cultural fabric of the Cotswolds.

Roses Theatre (Tewkesbury):

Situated amidst the picturesque surroundings of Tewkesbury, the Roses Theatre exudes a distinct charm that perfectly complements the town's historic ambiance. This cultural haven stands as a testament to the enduring vitality of the performing arts in the region. The Roses Theatre is celebrated for its eclectic program of events, which encompasses live theater productions, captivating cinema screenings, and mesmerizing musical performances.

The theater's repertoire of live productions spans an impressive range of genres and styles, ensuring that audiences are treated to a rich tapestry of storytelling. Whether it's the evocative portrayal of a classic play, the exuberant energy of a contemporary piece, or the whimsical charm of a family-friendly show, the Roses Theatre endeavors to cater to a diverse audience. Additionally, the theater offers a cinematic experience like no other, with carefully curated film screenings that range from critically acclaimed releases to timeless classics. The inclusion of musical performances adds an extra layer of enchantment to the theater's offerings, providing a platform for local and visiting musicians to showcase their talents.

The Theatre Chipping Norton:

Nestled in the heart of Chipping Norton, this intimate theater embodies the very essence of Cotswold charm. Its unassuming exterior belies the treasure trove of artistic brilliance that lies within. The Theatre Chipping Norton stands as a true gem, offering a distinctive cultural experience that is cherished by both locals and visitors alike.

Within its walls, patrons are treated to an eclectic mix of theatrical delights. From thought-provoking plays that challenge the intellect to uproarious comedy shows that leave audiences in fits of laughter, the theater's programming is a testament to its dedication to providing a diverse and enriching cultural experience. Live music events further enhance the theater's offerings, with a lineup that spans various genres and styles, ensuring there's something to captivate every musical palate.

In conclusion, the Everyman Theatre in Cheltenham, the Roses Theatre in Tewkesbury, and The Theatre Chipping Norton are not mere venues; they are cultural beacons that illuminate the Cotswolds with the brilliance of the performing arts. Their dedication to curating diverse and captivating programs is a testament to their significance in the region's cultural landscape. These theaters stand as testaments to the enduring power of the arts and their ability to inspire, entertain, and enrich the lives of all who have the privilege of experiencing their offerings.

7.2 Nightclubs and Lounges

For those seeking a lively nightlife experience, the Cotswolds doesn't disappoint. While it's not known for its clubbing scene, there are plenty of cozy lounges and pubs that offer a perfect setting for a night out. Some favorites include:

MooMoo Clubrooms (Cheltenham):

Location: 16 Regent St, Cheltenham GL50 1HE

Description: A popular nightclub in Cheltenham known for its dynamic atmosphere, live DJs, and themed nights. It's a go-to spot for those seeking an energetic nightlife experience.

Subtone (Cheltenham):

Location: 21-27 St James's Square, Cheltenham GL50 3PR

Description: An underground venue in Cheltenham celebrated for its eclectic music playlists and vibrant crowd. It offers an immersive experience for music enthusiasts.

Kings Head (Cirencester):

Location: 24 Market Pl, Cirencester GL7 2NR

Description: A historic pub in Cirencester that provides a laid-back yet lively atmosphere. It's a favorite choice for those seeking a casual night out with friends.

Subtone (Cheltenham):

Location: 21-27 St James's Square, Cheltenham GL50 3PR

Description: An underground venue in Cheltenham celebrated for its eclectic music playlists and vibrant crowd. It offers an immersive experience for music enthusiasts.

Bamboo Club (Cheltenham):

Location: 15 Montpellier Walk, Cheltenham GL50 1SD

Description: A stylish nightclub in Cheltenham known for its exotic decor, top-notch DJs, and a range of music genres. It's a favorite for those seeking a chic and lively atmosphere.

Vinestock (Stow-on-the-Wold):

Location: Talbot Court, Sheep St, Stow-on-the-Wold GL54 1BQ

Description: A wine bar and lounge in Stow-on-the-Wold, known for its extensive wine selection, relaxed ambiance, and occasional live music. It's a great place for a sophisticated evening out.

The Hollow Bottom (Guiting Power):

Location: Guiting Power, Cheltenham GL54 5UX

Description: A charming pub in Guiting Power, known for its cozy atmosphere and occasional live music sessions. It's a local favorite for a relaxed night out.

Please note that it's always a good idea to check the opening hours and any special events or themed nights before planning your visit.

7.3 Family-Friendly Entertainment
Cotswold Wildlife Park and Gardens (Burford):

Nestled in the heart of the Cotswolds, the Cotswold Wildlife Park and Gardens stands as a beacon of natural wonder, offering families a day of exploration and excitement. This sprawling park is a treasure trove of biodiversity, housing an extensive array of animals from across the globe. From the majestic grace of giraffes to the playful antics of lemurs, the park provides an up-close encounter with creatures both familiar and exotic.

In addition to its captivating animal exhibits, the park boasts beautifully landscaped gardens that provide a serene backdrop to the wildlife spectacle. Immaculately maintained, these gardens offer a tranquil space for families to wander, relax, and appreciate the harmony of nature. Children will delight in exploring the various play areas scattered throughout the park, designed to ignite their imagination and energy.

Corinium Museum (Cirencester):

For families seeking an intellectual adventure, the Corinium Museum in Cirencester is a captivating destination. This interactive museum invites visitors on a journey through the rich tapestry of Cotswold history. The exhibits are thoughtfully curated to engage visitors of all ages, with a particular focus on providing a hands-on experience for children.

Young historians can unearth ancient artifacts, try their hand at archaeological discovery, and even step into the shoes of Roman citizens in the museum's reconstructions. The Corinium Museum's educational approach ensures that families leave not only entertained but also enriched with a deeper understanding of the region's cultural heritage.

Adam Henson's Cotswold Farm Park (Guiting Power):

Nestled amidst the rolling hills of Guiting Power, Adam Henson's Cotswold Farm Park offers families an authentic farm experience that's both educational and immensely enjoyable. This working farm is a living testament to the agricultural traditions of the Cotswolds. Children have the opportunity to interact with a menagerie of friendly animals, from fluffy lambs to curious piglets.

The farm's ethos is rooted in hands-on learning, and children are encouraged to participate in various activities, including animal feeding sessions and informative talks about farm life. Additionally, the park features outdoor play areas and nature trails, allowing young adventurers to burn off energy while exploring the natural beauty that surrounds them.

In conclusion, the Cotswolds are more than just a picturesque backdrop for family holidays. They offer a wealth of engaging activities that cater to the interests of both children and parents. Whether it's a day of wildlife discovery at the Cotswold Wildlife Park and Gardens, an educational journey through history at the Corinium Museum, or an immersive farm experience at Adam Henson's Cotswold Farm Park, families are sure to create cherished memories that will last a lifetime. These family-friendly attractions embody the essence of the Cotswolds - a place where natural beauty, cultural heritage, and joyful experiences converge to create lasting impressions for visitors of all ages.

7.4 Special Events and Festivals

Throughout the year, the Cotswolds hosts an array of special events and festivals that showcase the region's culture, traditions, and local talents. Some noteworthy events include:

Cheltenham Literature Festival:

The Cheltenham Literature Festival stands as a testament to the enduring power of words and ideas. Recognized worldwide, it is a celebration of literature that draws bibliophiles, thinkers, and creatives from every corner of the globe. The festival's legacy stretches back decades, marking its place as one of the most significant literary events on the calendar.

Throughout the festival, the town of Cheltenham is transformed into a hive of intellectual activity. The streets buzz with excitement as attendees gather to immerse themselves in a diverse program of talks, discussions, workshops, and lectures. Acclaimed authors, poets, philosophers, and cultural luminaries take center stage, sharing their insights, inspirations, and perspectives on a myriad of subjects.

One can expect a rich tapestry of genres, from fiction and non-fiction to poetry and philosophy. Each year, the festival's organizers curate a dynamic lineup that caters to a wide range of literary tastes and interests. Attendees have the opportunity not only to hear from their favorite writers but also to engage in lively debates, book signings, and interactive sessions that forge connections between authors and their readers.

The Cheltenham Literature Festival transcends the boundaries of a traditional literary event. It is a vibrant convergence of minds, a space where ideas are celebrated, challenged, and cherished. Whether one is an avid reader, a budding writer, or simply a lover of words, this festival is a pilgrimage that offers a profound and enriching experience. ·

Bourton-on-the-Water Football in the River:

Amidst the bucolic charm of Bourton-on-the-Water, a uniquely entertaining event unfolds: Football in the River. This spectacle is a testament to the Cotswolds' penchant for combining tradition with lighthearted revelry. Each year, teams gather on the banks of the tranquil River Windrush, ready to embark on a spirited game of football - in the water.

With the river as their pitch, players splash, kick, and maneuver their way towards victory, all while keeping their heads above water - both literally and figuratively. The event draws not only the local community but also curious spectators from far and wide, eager to witness this one-of-a-kind sporting extravaganza.

The jovial atmosphere is infectious, and laughter echoes across the riverbanks as players navigate the watery terrain with gusto. Children cheer from the sidelines, families gather for picnics, and visitors immerse themselves in the playful spirit of the occasion. Football in the River is a testament to the Cotswolds' ability to infuse tradition with a sense of whimsy, creating an event that is as entertaining as it is endearing.

Giffords Circus Tour:

Step into a world of enchantment with the Giffords Circus Tour, a vintage-style extravaganza that brings a touch of magic to the Cotswolds. This traveling circus is a spectacle of wonder and delight, captivating audiences of all ages with its nostalgic charm and captivating performances.

As the big top rises amidst the Cotswold countryside, it heralds the arrival of a troupe of talented performers, each an expert in their own unique art. Acrobats defy gravity, clowns provoke fits of laughter, and musicians serenade the audience with melodic tunes. The atmosphere is electric, a fusion of skill, artistry, and a touch of the unexpected.

Giffords Circus Tour is not merely a performance; it is an experience that transcends the boundaries of time. It harks back to an era when circuses were a grand affair, where the smell of popcorn mingled with the thrill of anticipation. Children gaze wide-eyed at the mesmerizing acts, while adults find themselves transported back to a time of innocence and wonder.

The tour weaves its way through various Cotswold locations, each venue providing a unique backdrop for this spectacle of entertainment. Families, couples, and friends gather under the canvas canopy, bound by a shared sense of awe and delight. The Giffords Circus Tour is a reminder that, even in the modern world, there is still magic to be found in the simplicity of a captivating performance. It is an experience that lingers in the hearts and memories of all who have the privilege of being part of this extraordinary event.

CHAPTER EIGHT

CULTURAL EXPERIENCES

8.1 Museums and Galleries

The Cotswolds boast a rich cultural heritage, which is beautifully preserved in its museums and galleries. From ancient artifacts to contemporary art, there's something to captivate every visitor:

Bourton House Garden Gallery (Bourton-on-the-Hill)

Nestled in the heart of the Cotswolds, the Bourton House Garden Gallery offers visitors a unique fusion of art and nature in a setting of unrivaled beauty. This gallery, situated within the enchanting Bourton House Garden, stands as a testament to the region's rich cultural tapestry. Local and international artists alike find inspiration in the captivating surroundings, contributing to an ever-evolving collection of masterpieces.

As you step into the gallery, the interplay between the art and the garden becomes immediately apparent. The carefully curated exhibits are thoughtfully arranged to harmonize with the natural elements outside. Paintings, sculptures, and other artistic expressions find their place among the vibrant flora and serene water features, creating a dynamic dialogue between human creativity and the splendors of nature.

The works displayed here range from classical to contemporary, each piece selected for its ability to resonate with the surroundings. Visitors may find themselves lost in the brushstrokes of a landscape painting, transported to a realm where the lines between art and reality blur. Sculptures, some intricately detailed and others boldly abstract, punctuate the gallery space, inviting contemplation and conversation.

Bourton House Garden Gallery is not only a celebration of visual art but also a testament to the enduring human desire to connect with the natural world. It is a place where creativity thrives in harmony with the seasons, where the changing light casts new perspectives on familiar pieces, and where the boundary between indoor and outdoor art dissolves into an immersive aesthetic experience.

Corinium Museum (Cirencester)

Stepping into the Corinium Museum is akin to embarking on a journey through time, delving deep into the historical tapestry of the Cotswolds. Situated in the ancient Roman town of Cirencester, this museum stands as a custodian of the region's rich heritage. Its exhibits, a carefully curated collection of artifacts and interactive displays, offer a window into the lives of those who walked these streets centuries ago.

The museum's crown jewel lies in its extensive Roman collection. Here, meticulously preserved artifacts tell the story of a bustling Roman town, once known as Corinium Dobunnorum. From intricately designed mosaics that adorned the floors of grand villas to everyday items like pottery and tools, each piece offers a glimpse into the daily lives, customs, and craftsmanship of this ancient civilization.

Beyond the Roman era, the Corinium Museum takes visitors on a chronological journey through time, unveiling the layers of history that have shaped the Cotswolds. Anglo-Saxon treasures, medieval relics, and Tudor-era curiosities all find their place within these walls. Interactive displays invite hands-on exploration, allowing visitors to engage with history in a tangible and memorable way.

The Corinium Museum is more than a repository of artifacts; it is a living testament to the enduring legacy of the Cotswolds. It invites us to reflect on the passage of time, to marvel at the ingenuity of those who came before us, and to gain a deeper appreciation for the layers of history that underlie the picturesque landscapes of the present day.

The Wilson Cheltenham Art Gallery & Museum (Cheltenham)

Situated in the elegant town of Cheltenham, The Wilson Cheltenham Art Gallery & Museum stands as a beacon of artistic expression in the heart of the Cotswolds. This cultural hub is a testament to the vibrant arts community that thrives in the region, showcasing a diverse collection of works that span genres, styles, and epochs.

The gallery spaces within The Wilson come alive with a dynamic interplay of artistic voices. Here, visitors can explore an extensive collection of paintings, sculptures, and mixed-media installations, each piece offering a unique perspective on the world. From the classical elegance of traditional portraiture to the bold experimentation of contemporary abstract art, the gallery's offerings are as diverse as the artists themselves.

In addition to its visual art collection, The Wilson is home to a wealth of historical artifacts and cultural exhibits. Visitors can immerse themselves in the stories of the Cotswolds, from its industrial heritage to its literary legacy. A special emphasis is placed on local artists, with the works of renowned Cotswold painters and sculptors taking center stage.

The Wilson Cheltenham Art Gallery & Museum is a space of inspiration and introspection, inviting visitors to engage with the boundless creativity of the human spirit. It is a celebration of artistic expression in all its forms, a testament to the enduring legacy of the Cotswolds as a crucible of creativity.

Cotswold Motoring Museum (Bourton-on-the-Water)

For aficionados of automotive history and enthusiasts of bygone eras, the Cotswold Motoring Museum in Bourton-on-the-Water is a treasure trove of nostalgia and engineering marvels. This captivating museum takes visitors on a journey through the evolution of transportation, from the earliest motor vehicles to the iconic cars of the mid-20th century.

As you step into the museum, you're greeted by a mesmerizing array of vintage cars, motorcycles, and automobilia. Each vehicle tells a story, reflecting the ingenuity and craftsmanship of its era. From the elegant curves of early 20th-century automobiles to the streamlined designs of post-war classics, the collection is a testament to the ever-evolving art of automotive engineering.

The exhibits are more than static displays; they're a living testament to the passion of collectors and restorers who have lovingly preserved these mechanical marvels. The museum's ambiance is enhanced by period settings, transporting visitors back in time to an era when motoring was as much about style and elegance as it was about functionality.

One of the highlights of the Cotswold Motoring Museum is its attention to detail. Interactive displays allow visitors to get hands-on with certain exhibits, providing a deeper understanding of the mechanics and innovations that shaped the automotive industry. It's a place where enthusiasts can revel in the nostalgia of a bygone motoring era.

Nature in Art (Wallsworth Hall, Twigworth)

Nestled within the idyllic surroundings of Wallsworth Hall in Twigworth, Nature in Art stands as a testament to the enduring connection between artistic expression and the natural world. As the world's first museum dedicated solely to art inspired by nature, it offers a unique perspective on the intersection of creativity and the environment.

The museum's collection is a celebration of the diverse forms that nature has inspired in artists throughout the ages. Paintings, sculptures, and crafts depict everything from the grandeur of landscapes to the intricate details of flora and fauna. Each piece is a testament to the awe-inspiring beauty and boundless diversity of the natural world.

What sets Nature in Art apart is its commitment to fostering a sense of wonder and conservation. The museum hosts workshops, exhibitions, and educational programs that inspire visitors to connect with nature on a deeper level.

Through art, it encourages a dialogue about environmental stewardship and the importance of preserving the world's biodiversity.

Visiting Nature in Art is a journey of discovery, a chance to see the world through the eyes of artists who find inspiration in the rhythms of nature. It invites us to reflect on our own relationship with the environment and to appreciate the delicate balance that sustains life on our planet. Nature in Art is a sanctuary for creativity, a place where art and nature converge in a symphony of color, form, and imagination.

8.2 Cultural Arts and Heritage

The Cotswolds' cultural arts and heritage are woven into the very fabric of the region. Here are some key aspects to explore:

Arts and Crafts Movement in the Cotswolds

The Cotswolds resonate with the profound influence of the Arts and Crafts Movement, a transformative cultural shift that championed the values of skillful craftsmanship, simplicity, and a return to age-old techniques. Spearheaded by luminaries like William Morris, this movement fervently advocated for the handmade, the unique, rejecting the impersonal uniformity of factory-produced goods. In this idyllic region, the Cotswolds became a haven for these ideals, nurturing an environment where artists, artisans, and craftspeople could not only thrive but also shape the very essence of the landscape.

Central to the Arts and Crafts ethos was the aspiration to infuse art seamlessly into the fabric of everyday life. Here in the Cotswolds, this philosophy is palpable in the minutest details of architecture, furniture, textiles, and myriad ordinary articles. The enduring legacy of Morris and his contemporaries manifests itself in the intricately carved ornamentation of historic edifices, the elaborate tapestries that grace the interiors, and the bespoke fixtures that embellish both private residences and public spaces.

However, the commitment of the Cotswolds to the Arts and Crafts Movement transcends the purely aesthetic realm; it embodies a way of life. Artisans and workshops, inspired by Morris' visionary principles, persist in the creation of exceptional, handcrafted goods. The discerning visitor can immerse themselves in a world of creativity by exploring the studios and galleries scattered throughout the region. Here, skilled craftspeople diligently hone their crafts, ensuring that the enduring influence of the Arts and Crafts Movement continues to shape and enrich the Cotswolds for generations to come. This dedication to preserving the authenticity and integrity of handcrafted work is not merely a nod to history, but a living, breathing testament to the enduring legacy of this artistic renaissance.

Festivals and Events: Celebrating Cotswold Culture

Immersing oneself in local traditions is a quintessential experience in the Cotswolds, and there's no better way to do so than by participating in the vibrant festivals and events that dot the calendar year-round. These gatherings offer a glimpse into the heart of Cotswold culture, where old customs meet contemporary celebrations.

The Cheltenham Literature Festival stands as a testament to the region's literary heritage. Hosting a stellar lineup of authors, poets, and thinkers, it's a celebration of words and ideas that has drawn literary enthusiasts from around the world. The Chipping Campden Music Festival, on the other hand, weaves a tapestry of melodies through the historic streets and churches of this picturesque town. It's a testament to the enduring power of music to unite communities and transcend generations.

Village fairs, with their array of stalls, games, and performances, capture the essence of rural life. These events harken back to a time when communities would come together to celebrate the harvest, share stories, and revel in each other's company. Attending a village fair is like stepping into a living storybook, where the past and present coalesce in a joyful celebration of community.

Cotswold Traditions: Timeless Customs and Celebrations

The Cotswolds are steeped in a tapestry of customs and celebrations that have been cherished for centuries. One such tradition is the heart-pounding spectacle of cheese rolling at Cooper's Hill. This gravity-defying race, where participants chase a wheel of cheese down a steep hill, is a testament to the region's irrepressible spirit and sense of adventure. It's an event that brings together locals and visitors alike in an adrenaline-fueled celebration of daring and camaraderie.

Ancient May Day celebrations, with their colorful processions, maypole dancing, and crowning of the May

Queen, offer a window into the region's pagan roots. These festivities mark the arrival of spring, a time of renewal and rebirth, and are a vivid reminder of the enduring connection between the people of the Cotswolds and the natural world.

Historic Architecture: Cotswold Stone Cottages and Manor Houses

The Cotswolds boast some of the most exquisite and well-preserved examples of historic architecture in England. The iconic Cotswold stone, with its warm, honeyed hue, graces cottages, manor houses, and churches alike. This distinctive building material, quarried locally, has been an integral part of the region's architectural identity for centuries.

As you wander through the picturesque villages of the Cotswolds, you'll encounter rows of charming stone cottages, their walls adorned with climbing roses and wisteria. Each dwelling is a testament to the skill and craftsmanship of the builders who, over the centuries, have created homes that harmonize seamlessly with the natural surroundings.

Manor houses, with their grand facades and sprawling gardens, offer a glimpse into the opulent lifestyles of the gentry who once called the Cotswolds home. These historic estates are living museums, preserving the stories and legacies of the families who shaped the region's history.

The churches of the Cotswolds, many of which date back to medieval times, are architectural marvels in their own right. From the grandeur of St. Mary's in Fairford to the simplicity of St. Barnabas' in Snowshill, these sacred spaces are a testament to the enduring faith and artistic prowess of generations past.

8.3 Understanding Local Customs and Tradition

To truly savor the essence of the Cotswolds, one must delve into the rich tapestry of customs and traditions that have shaped its character over centuries. These cultural threads, woven into the fabric of everyday life, offer a deeper connection to the region's heritage and a more profound appreciation of its unique charm.

Tea Time: A Quintessential Cotswold Experience

Engaging in the cherished English tradition of afternoon tea is a delightful way to immerse oneself in the Cotswold way of life. Afternoon tea is more than a meal; it's an institution, a cherished ritual of hospitality and conviviality. As you settle into a quaint tearoom, you'll be greeted by the comforting aroma of freshly brewed tea, typically served in elegant porcelain teapots. Accompanying this liquid refreshment are delectable treats, including scones adorned with clotted cream and fruit preserves, delicate finger sandwiches, and an assortment of pastries and cakes.

The Cotswolds take this tradition seriously, ensuring that every element of the experience is a celebration of quality and taste. The tea itself is often sourced from local providers, and the pastries and sandwiches are lovingly prepared with a commitment to both tradition and innovation. As you indulge in these culinary delights, you'll be enveloped in an atmosphere of refinement and relaxation, where time seems to slow down, allowing for meaningful conversation and connection.

Village Life: Warm Hospitality and Community Spirit

One of the most enchanting aspects of the Cotswolds is its charming villages, where warm hospitality and a strong sense of community prevail. To truly appreciate this aspect of Cotswold culture, take a leisurely stroll through one of these idyllic settlements.

As you wander through cobblestone streets lined with honey-colored cottages, you'll likely encounter friendly locals who are more than willing to engage in conversation and share stories about their beloved village. This connection with residents provides an intimate glimpse into the heart and soul of the Cotswolds, revealing the deep pride and affection they hold for their heritage.

It's not uncommon to find village pubs where the atmosphere is as inviting as the people. These historic establishments often serve as gathering places for locals and visitors alike, where you can enjoy a traditional British pint and engage in lively conversations that bridge cultures and generations.

Seasonal Celebrations: Vibrancy Amidst the Seasons

To experience the Cotswolds at its most vibrant, participate in the region's seasonal celebrations. Whether it's the festive Christmas markets, the lively summer fetes, or the bounteous harvest festivals, these events are a testament to the enduring spirit of the Cotswolds.

Christmas Markets: During the holiday season, Cotswold towns and villages transform into enchanting wonderlands, with Christmas markets taking center stage. Stroll through streets adorned with twinkling lights, explore artisanal stalls offering unique gifts and decorations, and savor seasonal treats like mulled wine and roasted chestnuts. The Cotswolds come alive with the magic of the season, creating a warm and festive atmosphere that's a joy to behold.

Summer Fetes: Summertime in the Cotswolds is synonymous with traditional village fetes. These quintessentially English events feature a delightful mix of activities, from fairground rides to homemade cakes and jams. You can try your hand at classic games like sack races or enjoy live music performances. The fetes provide a wonderful opportunity to interact with the locals and partake in the merriment of the season.

Harvest Festivals: In the autumn, the Cotswolds celebrate the harvest season with vibrant festivals that pay homage to the region's agricultural heritage. These festivals often feature colorful displays of locally grown produce, including pumpkins, apples, and more. It's a time to appreciate the bounty of the land and to revel in the sense of abundance that permeates the countryside.

In conclusion, the customs and traditions of the Cotswolds are an integral part of its allure. By participating in these cherished practices, from the elegance of afternoon tea to the warmth of village life and the vibrancy of seasonal celebrations, visitors can gain a deeper understanding of the region's cultural richness and its welcoming embrace of all who are fortunate enough to experience it.

CHAPTER NINE

OUTDOOR ACTIVITIES

9.1 Hiking Trails and Walks

The Cotswolds, a patchwork of rolling hills, ancient woodlands, and charming villages, offer a myriad of hiking opportunities for enthusiasts of all levels. Whether you're seeking a leisurely stroll through picturesque hamlets or a challenging trek along a historic trail, this region caters to every type of explorer.

At the heart of Cotswold hiking experiences lies the illustrious Cotswold Way, a trail that spans an impressive 102 miles (164 km) from the idyllic town of Chipping Campden to the historic city of Bath. Renowned as one of England's most iconic long-distance footpaths, the Cotswold Way meanders through emerald-green hills, past time-honored sites, and unveils breathtaking vistas at every turn. Along its course, hikers are treated to a panorama of the Cotswolds' unrivaled beauty, encompassing rolling landscapes, ancient ruins, and an array of charming villages. Whether you embark on a grand adventure tackling the entire trail or opt for a more intimate exploration of select sections, the Cotswold Way guarantees an unforgettable journey, steeped in natural splendor and historical significance.

For those seeking a more concise yet equally enchanting experience, the Bredon Hill Circular Walk beckons. Covering a distance of 6.5 miles (10.5 km), this captivating trail introduces hikers to the Cotswolds' natural wonders in a condensed yet richly rewarding package. As you ascend towards the summit of Bredon Hill, nature's bounty unfolds around you, revealing sweeping vistas that stretch across the surrounding countryside. It's an awe-inspiring vantage point that allows you to fully appreciate the Cotswolds' undulating terrain, adorned with patchwork fields and punctuated by charming villages. Additionally, this circular route guides you past the remnants of an ancient Iron Age hill fort, serving as a poignant reminder of the region's deep-rooted historical tapestry. The walk provides a vivid window into a bygone era, allowing you to touch the vestiges of ancient civilizations that once thrived in this picturesque landscape.

Intriguingly, the trail also invites you to immerse yourself in the Cotswolds' rich biodiversity. Diverse flora and fauna grace the path, creating a sensory tapestry that further enhances the experience. The symphony of birdsong, the subtle rustling of leaves, and the fragrance of wildflowers infuse the air, creating an atmosphere of natural harmony.

Whether you're embarking on a grand odyssey along the Cotswold Way or embarking on the intimate Bredon Hill Circular Walk, the Cotswolds beckon with open arms, inviting you to step into a world of captivating landscapes, ancient history, and vibrant biodiversity. Each step taken in this idyllic countryside is a stride toward a deeper appreciation of nature's enduring beauty and the rich tapestry of human history that graces this remarkable region.

9.2 Cycling Routes and Tours

For cycling enthusiasts, the Cotswolds present a veritable playground of possibilities, offering a diverse range of routes that cater to all levels of riders. From leisurely journeys through idyllic villages to exhilarating hill climbs, this region is a haven for those who seek to explore its scenic beauty on two wheels. Whether you bring your own bicycle or choose to rent one, the Cotswolds beckon with an invitation to embark on an adventure that unfolds at your own pace, with every pedal stroke revealing a new facet of this captivating landscape.

Cotswold Water Park: Where Nature Meets Adventure

Spanning a diverse array of landscapes, the Cotswold Water Park is a cyclist's dream come true. With an extensive network of trails that weave around the park's numerous lakes, this destination offers something for cyclists of every caliber. The distances vary, ensuring that whether you're a casual rider or a seasoned pro, you'll find a route that suits your preference.

The park's charm lies not only in its cycling opportunities, but also in the rich tapestry of natural wonders it encompasses. Here, you'll have the chance to encounter an array of wildlife, from graceful waterfowl to elusive otters, adding a touch of enchantment to your journey. And should you wish to pause and soak in the surroundings, the lakesides provide perfect spots for a leisurely picnic, where the soothing sounds of nature form a serene backdrop to your reprieve.

Cotswold Villages Tour: A Guided Journey through Time

For those seeking a curated cycling experience, the Cotswold Villages Tour is an absolute must. This customizable tour invites you to delve into the heart of the region's quintessential villages, each one steeped in centuries of history and culture. Led by knowledgeable guides, you'll navigate the narrow country lanes that wind through these picturesque hamlets, uncovering hidden treasures and absorbing the tales that echo through cobblestone streets.

Along the way, historic landmarks stand as living testaments to the Cotswolds' enduring legacy. Time-worn churches, charming thatched cottages, and market squares steeped in tradition provide windows into a bygone era. Your guides, passionate about the area's cultural heritage, will regale you with stories and insights, painting vivid pictures of the lives that once thrived in these storied villages.

As you pedal through this living tapestry of history, each turn offers a new discovery, a fresh perspective on a landscape that seems plucked from the pages of a storybook. Whether you're drawn to the enchanting beauty of Bourton-on-the-Water, the timeless elegance of Chipping Campden, or the historic allure of Stow-on-the-Wold, the Cotswold Villages Tour ensures you experience the essence of each village in all its unique splendor.

In the Cotswolds, cycling becomes an immersive experience, a means to not only traverse the landscape, but to engage with it on a profound level. It's a journey of discovery, where every mile brings a new revelation, and every village tells a new tale. From the tranquil serenity of the Water Park to the time-honored streets of the villages, each route offers its own distinct charm, inviting you to become a part of the Cotswolds' rich narrative. As you pedal along, you'll find that this region has a way of leaving an indelible mark on the soul, a testament to the enduring allure of this remarkable corner of England.

9.3 Birdwatching and Wildlife Encounters

In the heart of the Cotswolds, nature unveils its grandeur in a display of rich biodiversity that thrives amidst the picturesque landscapes. Beyond the rolling hills and charming villages, this region is a sanctuary for birdwatchers and wildlife enthusiasts seeking to witness nature in all its unspoiled glory.

Slimbridge Wetland Centre: A Symphony of Feathers

Highlights: Diverse bird species, wetland habitats.

Nestled within the embrace of the Wildfowl and Wetlands Trust, Slimbridge Wetland Centre stands as a testament to the vibrant avian life that graces the Cotswolds. This haven for birdwatchers unfolds across a tapestry of habitats, each one a vital ecosystem that sustains a diverse array of bird species. Marshes, lagoons, and reedbeds form a complex mosaic, providing a refuge for both resident and migratory waterfowl.

Here, the air is alive with the calls and songs of countless birds, creating a symphony of nature that serenades visitors as they explore the wetland trails. From the graceful wading birds that stalk the shallows to the vibrant waterfowl that dance upon the ponds, Slimbridge offers a front-row seat to the intricacies of avian life. With binoculars in hand, visitors can observe these winged wonders in their natural habitat, gaining a deeper appreciation for their behaviors and interactions.

Cotswold Falconry Centre: A Dance of Raptors

Highlights: Birds of prey, interactive displays.

For those who yearn for a more intimate encounter with nature's aerial marvels, the Cotswold Falconry Centre beckons. Here, the focus shifts to the powerful and majestic birds of prey that rule the skies. Visitors have the unique opportunity to stand in the presence of owls, falcons, and eagles, marveling at the fierce beauty that defines these creatures.

Expert falconers guide the experience, sharing their passion and knowledge of these magnificent birds. Through interactive displays, visitors gain insight into the behaviors, hunting techniques, and adaptations that allow raptors to thrive in their respective environments. The sheer power and grace exhibited during flying demonstrations are nothing short of mesmerizing, leaving an indelible impression of the natural world's extraordinary diversity.

This hands-on encounter with birds of prey offers a profound connection to the wild. As visitors witness the primal instincts and keen intelligence of these creatures, they gain a deeper understanding of the delicate balance that exists within ecosystems. It's a rare opportunity to bridge the gap between human and wildlife, forging a connection that lingers long after the visit.

In the Cotswolds, nature reveals itself in all its splendor, inviting those with a love for wildlife to step into a world of feathers and flight. From the tranquil wetlands of Slimbridge to the exhilarating displays at the Cotswold Falconry Centre, each encounter offers a glimpse into the intricate tapestry of life that thrives in this region. Whether you're an avid birdwatcher or simply a lover of the natural world, the Cotswolds beckon with open arms, promising an immersive journey into the heart of untamed beauty. Here, nature's bounty is not merely observed, but experienced, leaving an indelible mark on the soul and a lasting appreciation for the wonder that is the Cotswolds.

CHAPTER TEN

HIDDEN GEMS AND BEYOND

10.1 Secret Spots and Lesser-Known Attractions

While the Cotswolds boast well-known attractions, there are hidden gems waiting to be discovered by the discerning traveler. Here are a few secret spots that promise a unique experience:

1. The Rollright Stones Revisited

Nestled in the Heart of the Cotswolds

As you meander through the picturesque landscapes of the Cotswolds, where charming villages and lush green hills dominate the scene, it's easy to get swept up in the region's well-known attractions. Yet, for those with a keen sense of adventure and an appetite for history, there exists a hidden gem that promises to transport you through time and ignite your imagination: The Rollright Stones.

A Mystical History Beckons

The Rollright Stones, located in the heart of the Cotswolds, offer a unique and mystical journey into the past. Unlike some of the more famous stone circles in the UK, such as Stonehenge or Avebury, the Rollright Stones remain off the beaten path, making them a tranquil haven for those in search of a more intimate encounter with ancient history.

The Enigmatic Stones

At first glance, the Rollright Stones might not appear as grandiose as their renowned counterparts, but they possess an enigmatic charm that's just as compelling. This ancient stone circle is actually composed of three distinct groups of stones: the King's Men stone circle, the Whispering Knights dolmen, and the King Stone, each with its own fascinating history and legends.

The King's Men Stone Circle

Standing sentinel in the heart of the site is the King's Men stone circle. Comprising approximately 77 weathered stones, this circle exudes an air of mystery. Some believe that it was a burial or ceremonial site, while others speculate about its astronomical significance. What is certain is that it has stood for centuries, silently witnessing the passage of time and the changing landscape around it.

The Whispering Knights Dolmen

Just a stone's throw away from the King's Men circle lies the Whispering Knights dolmen. This burial chamber, believed to date back to the Early Neolithic period, is an eerie and evocative reminder of our distant ancestors. The stones seem to huddle together in conspiratorial conversation, giving rise to the name "Whispering Knights."

The King Stone

The third component of the Rollright Stones is the King Stone, which stands alone a short distance from the other two groups. This solitary monolith is thought to have once been part of a stone avenue leading to the King's Men circle. According to folklore, it was a king turned to stone by a witch's curse. Touching the King Stone is said to bring good luck, but it's also believed that it might be disastrous for anyone daring to move it.

Myth and Legend

No visit to the Rollright Stones is complete without delving into the rich tapestry of myths and legends that shroud these ancient monoliths. One of the most enduring stories is that of the witch who turned a king and his army to stone. The King Stone, according to local legend, is the king himself, and the King's Men are his soldiers, while the Whispering Knights are the treacherous knights who conspired with the witch.

Embracing Tranquility

One of the most remarkable aspects of the Rollright Stones is the sense of tranquility that envelops the site. Unlike more crowded tourist destinations, here you can immerse yourself in the quietude of the Cotswold countryside and reflect upon the mysteries of the past. The stones themselves seem to exude an aura of serenity, inviting you to pause and contemplate the centuries that have passed since they were first erected.

Walking in the Footsteps of History

Exploring the Rollright Stones is akin to taking a step back in time. As you wander among the ancient stones, you can't help but marvel at the skill and determination of the people who erected them. These stones have borne witness to countless generations, and by visiting them, you become a part of that timeless narrative.

Visiting the Rollright Stones

The Rollright Stones are open to the public throughout the year, and a modest admission fee helps support the preservation of this historic site. While the stones are accessible at any time, consider visiting during the quieter hours of the morning or late afternoon to fully appreciate the tranquility of the site.

Getting There

The Rollright Stones are conveniently located in the heart of the Cotswolds, making them easily accessible by car or public transportation. If you're driving, you'll find ample parking nearby. Alternatively, you can opt for public transport, with bus routes serving nearby towns like Chipping Norton and Moreton-in-Marsh.

A Timeless Experience

A visit to the Rollright Stones is more than just a historical outing; it's an opportunity to connect with the deep roots of the Cotswolds and to ponder the mysteries of the past. As you stand among these ancient stones, you can almost hear the whispers of history and the echoes of legends, making this lesser-visited site an essential stop on your Cotswolds journey. So, set aside a few hours, embrace the tranquility, and embark on a mystical adventure to the heart of the Cotswolds. The Rollright Stones await, ready to share their secrets with those who are willing to listen.

2. Coln Valley's Hidden Waterfalls

Escape to the Secluded Coln Valley

Nestled in the heart of the Cotswolds lies a well-kept secret, known only to a fortunate few. The Coln Valley, with its rolling hills and meandering streams, is a sanctuary of serenity. Among its many treasures, a series of enchanting waterfalls await, offering a refreshing detour from the well-trodden paths of more popular attractions.

A Symphony of Nature's Own Making

As you venture deeper into the Coln Valley, the soothing sound of rushing water becomes your guide. The melody of nature's symphony grows louder, drawing you closer to the hidden waterfalls. Surrounded by lush vegetation, the falls cascade down the ancient stone, creating a mesmerizing display of motion and grace.

A Treasured Secret

Coln Valley's waterfalls are a well-kept secret, known intimately by locals who cherish this tranquil oasis. Away from the bustling crowds, you'll find a sense of seclusion that allows you to fully immerse yourself in the natural beauty of the Cotswolds. It's a place where time seems to slow, and the worries of the world fade away, leaving only the purest connection with the natural world.

A Serene Journey

To reach the waterfalls, you'll embark on a serene journey through the Coln Valley. The path meanders along the banks of the river, offering glimpses of wildlife and the gentle rustling of leaves in the breeze. It's a walk that encourages contemplation and reflection, a chance to escape the demands of modern life and simply be present in the moment.

Enchanting Cascades

As you approach the waterfalls, the air becomes charged with anticipation. The first glimpse of the cascading water is nothing short of enchanting. Each tier of the falls reveals a new facet of its beauty, as the water gracefully descends, creating pools of crystalline clarity. The moss-covered rocks and vibrant flora surrounding the falls add to the ethereal atmosphere, painting a picture of untouched natural splendor.

A Place of Solace and Reverie

Coln Valley's hidden waterfalls invite you to linger, to find a quiet spot along the riverbank and let the sights and sounds envelop you. It's a place of solace, where the worries of the world seem to fade into the background. The rushing water becomes a soothing lullaby, inviting you to close your eyes and simply be. Here, amidst the beauty of the Cotswolds, you can find a sense of peace that transcends the ordinary.

Respecting Nature's Sanctuary

As you revel in the beauty of the waterfalls, it's essential to remember that this is a place of delicate balance. Leave no trace of your visit, and tread lightly to preserve the natural integrity of the area. By respecting this sanctuary, you ensure that future generations can also experience the wonder of Coln Valley's hidden waterfalls.

Planning Your Visit

Visiting Coln Valley's hidden waterfalls is a rewarding endeavor, but it's important to plan accordingly. The path to the falls may require sturdy footwear and a moderate level of fitness. Be sure to check local guides or seek advice from knowledgeable locals for the best routes and any additional considerations.

A Timeless Experience

Coln Valley's hidden waterfalls offer more than just a beautiful sight—they provide an opportunity to connect with the raw, untamed essence of nature. It's a place where time seems to stand still, allowing you to fully appreciate the wonder that surrounds you. As you leave this hidden gem behind, you carry with you not only the memory of the waterfalls but also a deeper connection to the natural world. Coln Valley's enchanting waterfalls are a testament to the enduring beauty of the Cotswolds, a reminder that there are still hidden wonders waiting to be discovered.

3. Tucked Away near Winchcombe

In the quiet countryside near Winchcombe, a gem of history lies hidden amidst the Cotswolds' rolling hills. The hauntingly beautiful ruins of Hailes Abbey stand as a testament to the passage of time and the enduring spirit of human endeavor. This lesser-known historical site beckons the curious traveler to step back in time and immerse themselves in a world long gone.

A Serene Ambiance of Remnants

As you approach the ruins of Hailes Abbey, a sense of reverence washes over you. The remnants of this once thriving Cistercian monastery rise from the earth, their ancient stones weathered by centuries of wind and rain. The abbey's skeletal form against the backdrop of the lush Cotswold landscape creates a hauntingly beautiful tableau, inviting contemplation and reflection.

A Window into Centuries Past

Founded in the early 13th century, Hailes Abbey was a center of spiritual devotion and a place of respite for pilgrims. Its history is woven into the fabric of medieval England, and the abbey played a significant role in the religious and cultural tapestry of the time. The ruins now stand as a silent witness to the passing of centuries, offering visitors a precious window into a world that has long since faded into the annals of history.

The Echoes of Devotion

As you explore the abbey's remains, you can almost hear the echoes of the monks' chants and the hushed prayers of pilgrims who sought solace within these walls. The stone arches that still stand tall evoke a sense of reverence and a deep appreciation for the craftsmanship of those who built this sacred sanctuary.

A True Hidden Treasure

Hailes Abbey, though less frequented by tourists, holds a unique allure for those who seek a deeper connection with history. Unlike larger, more crowded attractions, here you can revel in the tranquility of the site, allowing the whispers of the past to carry you back in time. It's a true hidden treasure, cherished by those who understand the value of uncovering the lesser-known gems that dot the landscape.

The Fragility of History

As you walk through the abbey's ruins, it's impossible not to feel a profound sense of the impermanence of human endeavors. The once-grand structure, now reduced to fragments of its former glory, serves as a poignant reminder of the transience of all things. Yet, in its quiet decay, there is a beauty that speaks to the resilience of the human spirit and the enduring legacy of those who came before us.

Visiting Hailes Abbey

To visit Hailes Abbey is to embark on a journey through time. The site is open to the public, and a small fee supports its ongoing preservation. As you wander through the abbey, consider taking a moment to sit amidst the ruins, allowing the atmosphere to envelop you. It's a place where contemplation comes naturally, and where the stories of the past seem to come alive in the quiet whispers of the wind.

A Timeless Experience

Hailes Abbey stands as a testament to the rich history that permeates every corner of the Cotswolds. It invites you to step off the beaten path and immerse yourself in a world that exists at the intersection of past and present. As you bid farewell to this hauntingly beautiful site, you carry with you not only memories of the abbey itself, but also a deeper appreciation for the layers of history that define the Cotswolds. Hailes Abbey is a hidden treasure, waiting to be discovered by those who are willing to listen to its stories and heed its silent wisdom.

10.2 Charming Hamlets and Remote Retreats

The Cotswolds' charm extends beyond its popular villages. Venture to these tranquil hamlets and remote retreats for an intimate encounter with the region's rustic beauty:

1. Snowshill: Quintessential Cotswold Seclusion

Nestled in the Hills

In the heart of the Cotswolds, where the landscape unfurls in a patchwork of emerald fields and honey-hued cottages, lies the picturesque hamlet of Snowshill. Tucked away in the hills, Snowshill exudes an old-world charm that transports visitors to a time of simple beauty and rural tranquility. This hidden gem invites you to explore its cobbled streets and immerse yourself in the idyllic countryside that embraces it.

A Glimpse into Timeless Beauty

As you approach Snowshill, the sight that unfolds before you is nothing short of enchanting. The cottages, their golden stones aglow in the sunlight, exude a warmth and character that is quintessentially Cotswold. Each dwelling seems to have its own story to tell, its own secrets to share with those who care to listen.

Strolling Through Cobbled Streets

One of the true pleasures of visiting Snowshill is the opportunity to wander its cobbled streets at a leisurely pace.

The absence of bustling crowds allows you to soak in the atmosphere at your own rhythm. Every corner turned reveals a new vista, a new angle from which to admire the timeless beauty of this hamlet.

The Old Stone Manor

At the heart of Snowshill stands the grandeur of Snowshill Manor, a testament to centuries gone by. The manor's stone facade is adorned with ivy, and its mullioned windows seem to gaze out over the village with a watchful eye. As you explore the manor's interior, you're greeted by a collection of treasures amassed by Charles Wade, the man who lovingly restored the property in the early 20th century. Each room tells a story, offering a glimpse into the passions and curiosities of a bygone era.

Embraced by Idyllic Countryside

Surrounding Snowshill is a landscape of unrivaled beauty. The hills roll gently, their contours softened by fields of wildflowers and grazing sheep. It's a scene that seems lifted from the pages of a storybook, inviting you to breathe in the crisp, clean air and revel in the sense of peace that permeates the countryside.

A Living Testament to Cotswold Traditions

Snowshill is a place where time seems to stand still, preserving the traditions and way of life that define the Cotswolds. Here, you'll find the quintessential English village, complete with a medieval church, a cozy pub, and a sense of community that harks back to simpler times.

A Retreat from the Ordinary

For those seeking respite from the demands of modern life, Snowshill is a haven of tranquility. The absence of bustling tourist crowds means you can truly unwind and appreciate the subtle details that make this hamlet so special. The gentle rustling of leaves in the breeze, the distant chiming of church bells, and the occasional greeting from a passing local create a sense of retreat from the ordinary.

The Art of Doing Nothing

In Snowshill, there's a certain art to doing nothing at all. You might find yourself sitting on a bench, gazing out over the fields, lost in thought. Or perhaps you'll choose to savor a cup of tea outside a quaint tearoom, the minutes slipping by in unhurried contentment. It's a place where simply being is enough.

A Timeless Treasure

Snowshill is more than a village; it's a living testament to the enduring charm of the Cotswolds. It invites you to step into a world where simplicity reigns and beauty is found in every nook and cranny. As you bid farewell to this hidden hamlet, you carry with you not only memories of its cobbled streets and honeyed cottages, but also a deeper appreciation for the timeless allure of the Cotswolds. Snowshill is a place that lingers in the heart, a reminder that true beauty is often found in the most unassuming of places.

2. Lower Slaughter: A Riverside Haven

A Picturesque Escape

Nestled along the tranquil banks of the River Eye in the heart of the Cotswolds, Lower Slaughter stands as a testament to the timeless beauty of rural England. This lesser-visited gem, often overshadowed by its more famous neighbors, exudes a quiet charm that captivates those who venture here. With its meandering river and historic mill, Lower Slaughter beckons you to experience a slice of paradise, far removed from the hustle and bustle of modern life.

The Serenity of the River

As you approach Lower Slaughter, the gentle murmur of the River Eye welcomes you. This meandering waterway is the lifeblood of the village, its clear waters reflecting the surrounding greenery like a mirror. Along its banks, ducks and swans glide gracefully, creating a scene that seems plucked from a storybook.

Historic Mill and Riverside Cottages

At the heart of Lower Slaughter stands the iconic water mill, its waterwheel turning with a rhythmic precision that has endured for generations. This historic structure, adorned with cascades of ivy, serves as a reminder of the village's industrial past. The mill's warm golden hue complements the honeyed stone cottages that line the river, their thatched roofs adding a touch of rustic charm to the scene.

A Journey Back in Time

Walking through Lower Slaughter feels like stepping back in time. The village maintains an air of peaceful seclusion, with narrow, winding lanes that invite exploration. Each corner turned reveals a new delight—a centuries-old cottage with a blooming garden, a stone footbridge that spans the river, or a glimpse of the picturesque church steeple.

The Allure of Rural Paradise

Lower Slaughter embodies the quintessential English countryside—a place where time moves at a slower pace, and the natural beauty of the surroundings takes center stage. It's an invitation to pause, to breathe deeply of the fresh country air, and to appreciate the simple pleasures that this riverside haven offers.

The Stroll of Contemplation

A leisurely stroll along the riverbank is an experience to be savored in Lower Slaughter. The path takes you past charming stone cottages, their gardens bursting with vibrant blooms. The gentle sound of water flowing and birdsong creates a soundtrack that complements the serenity of the scene. It's a moment for quiet contemplation, a chance to appreciate the natural harmony that defines this picturesque village.

A Place for Nature's Whisper

In Lower Slaughter, nature is not a distant observer, but an active participant in the village's charm. The trees that line the river sway in gentle rhythm with the breeze, and the wildflowers that adorn the banks paint the landscape with a kaleidoscope of colors. It's a place where the boundary between man-made and natural beauty blurs, creating an atmosphere of seamless integration.

A Hidden Gem Worth Discovering

Lower Slaughter may be a lesser-visited destination, but it is undoubtedly a hidden gem of the Cotswolds. Here, amidst the timeless beauty of the countryside, you'll find a refuge from the demands of modern life. It's a place that invites you to linger, to absorb the tranquility, and to appreciate the intricate details that make this village so special.

Embracing Lower Slaughter

Whether you choose to explore the historic mill, wander the cobbled streets, or simply sit by the river and let the world pass by, Lower Slaughter offers an experience that lingers in the memory. As you bid farewell to this riverside haven, you carry with you not only the visual beauty of the village, but also a sense of peace and contentment—a reminder that true paradise can often be found in the most unexpected places. Lower Slaughter is a testament to the enduring allure of the Cotswolds, a place that welcomes all who seek solace in its idyllic embrace.

3. Bibury Meadows: A Hidden Riverside Retreat

A Hidden Riverside Retreat

Tucked away in the heart of the Cotswolds, beyond the charming lanes of the renowned Arlington Row, lies a hidden gem waiting to be discovered: Bibury Meadows. This lesser-known area offers a serene escape, inviting visitors to immerse themselves in the tranquility of the River Coln's gentle flow.

A Sanctuary of Calm

As you venture to Bibury Meadows, the world seems to slow down. The air is scented with the sweet fragrance of wildflowers, and the sound of birdsong creates a natural symphony that lulls you into a state of peaceful contemplation. Here, amidst the idyllic countryside, you'll find a sanctuary of calm that offers respite from the demands of everyday life.

Riverside Bliss

The star of Bibury Meadows is undoubtedly the River Coln, whose crystal-clear waters meander lazily through the meadows. The river's gentle flow is an invitation to simply be—to sit on its banks, toes grazing the cool water, and let the cares of the world drift away. It's a place where time seems to stand still, allowing you to fully appreciate the beauty that surrounds you.

A Patchwork of Natural Beauty

The meadows themselves are a tapestry of vibrant greens and golden hues, dotted with an array of wildflowers that sway in the breeze. The landscape is alive with the hum of bees and the occasional flutter of butterflies, creating a living canvas of nature's finest work. It's a place where every step is a testament to the harmonious relationship between man and the natural world.

The Charms of Arlington Row

Just a stone's throw away from Bibury Meadows lies the iconic Arlington Row, one of the most photographed spots in the Cotswolds. Its rows of picturesque cottages, each with its own unique character, exude a timeless charm. Strolling along this historic street, you can't help but feel a sense of connection to the generations that have walked these cobbles before you.

A Lesser-Known Treasure

While Arlington Row may draw the attention of many visitors, Bibury Meadows remains a lesser-known treasure, cherished by those who have uncovered its quiet allure. The absence of crowds allows you to explore at your own pace, to find a secluded spot along the riverbank, and to let the beauty of the surroundings wash over you.

The Dance of Light and Water

As the sun dances on the surface of the River Coln, casting dappled patterns of light and shadow, you can't help but feel a profound sense of gratitude for the simple pleasures of life. The ripples in the water create a soothing rhythm that lulls you into a state of peaceful reflection. It's a reminder that true luxury can often be found in the most uncomplicated moments.

The Melody of Nature

In Bibury Meadows, the melody of nature is ever-present. The whispering leaves, the gentle rustle of grasses, and the distant call of birds create a symphony that surrounds you. It's a melody that invites you to tune in, to let go of distractions, and to be fully present in the moment.

Embracing the Essence of Bibury Meadows

To visit Bibury Meadows is to experience a side of the Cotswolds that goes beyond the postcard-perfect scenes. It's a place where nature and history intertwine, where the river tells its own story of time's passage. As you bid farewell to this hidden riverside retreat, you carry with you not only the visual beauty of the meadows and the river, but also a sense of inner calm—a reminder that in the heart of the Cotswolds, there exists a sanctuary of serenity waiting to be discovered. Bibury Meadows is an invitation to reconnect with nature, to find solace in its embrace, and to carry that sense of peace with you long after you've left its shores.

10.3 Souvenirs and Mementos

Relive the magic of your Cotswolds adventure with these handpicked souvenirs, each a tangible piece of this captivating region's essence:

1. Cotswold Lavender Products

Evoke the scents of the rolling lavender fields with these exquisite lavender-infused products. Sourced from local farms, you'll find an array of delights, from fragrant oils to delicate sachets. With every whiff, you'll be transported back to the serene landscapes of the Cotswolds.

2. Artisanal Pottery from Cotswold Studios

Discover the artistry of the Cotswolds through unique pottery creations crafted by local artisans. Each piece bears the hallmark of handcrafted excellence, offering a tangible connection to the region's rich artistic heritage. From intricately designed mugs to elegantly glazed bowls, you're sure to find a piece that speaks to you.

3. Cotswold Honey and Beeswax Candles

Take a piece of the Cotswolds' natural bounty home with you. Locally-produced honey captures the essence of the region's flora and fauna, offering a sweet taste of its countryside. Complement this sensory delight with handcrafted beeswax candles, each one infused with the warm, golden glow of this cherished landscape.

These carefully selected souvenirs serve as more than mere mementos. They are tangible reminders of the beauty, tranquility, and craftsmanship that define the Cotswolds. Whether displayed in your home or savored in quiet moments, these treasures will forever hold the spirit of your Cotswolds journey.

CHAPTER ELEVEN

COTSWOLD TRAVEL ITINERARIES

11.1 One-Week Highlights Tour

Duration: 7 Days

Overview:

Embark on an unforgettable week-long journey through the heart of the Cotswolds, a region steeped in history, natural beauty, and timeless charm. The 'One-Week Highlights Tour' has been meticulously designed to encapsulate the very essence of this picturesque English countryside. Every day is a new chapter in this adventure, where you'll traverse through iconic landscapes, explore historic landmarks, and lose yourself in the quaint allure of villages that seem frozen in time.

Day 1: A Glimpse of Bibury

Your journey commences with a visit to the enchanting village of Bibury, often referred to as one of the most beautiful in England. Stroll along the idyllic Arlington Row, a row of 17th-century weaver's cottages that stand as a testament to the village's rich history. The gentle flow of the River Coln and the honey-hued stone buildings create a scene straight out of a postcard, offering a taste of the Cotswolds' quintessential charm.

Day 2: Castle Combe - The Quintessential Village

As the sun rises, you'll find yourself in Castle Combe, a village that has earned its reputation as the quintessential Cotswold village. The picturesque streets and medieval architecture exude a timeless aura. Take in the ambiance as you explore the nooks and crannies, and perhaps enjoy a cup of tea in a local tearoom. It's a day for immersion, a day to soak in the history that permeates every cobblestone.

Day 3: Blenheim Palace - A Palace Fit for Royalty

Today, you'll step into the grandeur of Blenheim Palace, a UNESCO World Heritage Site and the birthplace of Sir Winston Churchill. The palace's opulent architecture, set amidst meticulously landscaped gardens, tells a story of centuries gone by. Wander through the halls that have witnessed history, and stroll through the Capability Brown-designed parklands, breathing in the grandeur that defines this magnificent estate.

Day 4: Exploring Stow-on-the-Wold

The market town of Stow-on-the-Wold awaits, offering a fusion of history, culture, and natural beauty. Discover the imposing St. Edward's Church, a testament to medieval craftsmanship. The Market Square, with its array of charming shops and eateries, provides the perfect backdrop for a leisurely afternoon. As you wander, you'll find that every stone, every building, has a tale to tell.

Day 5: Chipping Campden - Tudor Charm in Abundance

Chipping Campden welcomes you with its stunning High Street, lined with honey-colored buildings that seem to glow in the sunlight. Here, you'll have the chance to explore Hidcote Manor Garden, a masterpiece of Arts and Crafts design. The intricacy of the garden's layout and the riot of colors make for an enchanting experience that showcases the beauty of nature in deliberate harmony.

Day 6: Discovering Bourton-on-the-Water

Known as the 'Venice of the Cotswolds', Bourton-on-the-Water beckons with its charming stone bridges that span the tranquil River Windrush. Enjoy a leisurely walk along the riverbanks, perhaps indulge in a riverside picnic, and explore the Cotswold Motoring Museum, a treasure trove of vintage automobiles and motoring memorabilia.

Day 7: Farewell to the Cotswolds

As your week-long adventure draws to a close, take a moment to reflect on the myriad experiences that have enriched your journey through the Cotswolds. Bid adieu to this enchanting region, knowing that the memories of its picturesque villages, historic landmarks, and breathtaking landscapes will remain etched in your heart forever.

This meticulously curated one-week highlights tour offers a taste of the Cotswolds' finest, inviting you to immerse yourself in the quintessential English countryside, where every turn reveals a new facet of beauty and history. It's a journey that leaves an indelible mark, a journey that invites you back to these timeless landscapes time and time again.

11.2 Two-Week Grand Tour

Overview:

Prepare to embark on an immersive journey through the heart of the Cotswolds. This meticulously crafted two-week grand tour offers an in-depth exploration of the hidden treasures that define this picturesque region. From the enchanting gardens of Hidcote Manor to the historic halls of Sudeley Castle, you'll have the opportunity to delve into the rich tapestry of culture and nature that graces the Cotswolds.

Day 1: Arrival in the Cotswolds

Your adventure begins with a warm welcome to the Cotswolds. After settling into your accommodation, take a leisurely stroll through the quaint streets of your chosen base. Allow yourself to acclimate to the idyllic surroundings, breathing in the fresh Cotswold air.

Day 2: Bibury and Arlington Row

Today, you'll have the pleasure of visiting Bibury, often hailed as one of England's most beautiful villages. As the morning mist lifts, stroll along Arlington Row, a collection of 17th-century weaver's cottages that stand as living testaments to the village's rich history. The river's gentle flow and the golden hue of the stone cottages create a mesmerizing scene that captures the very essence of the Cotswolds.

Day 3: Castle Combe - Timeless Charm

Castle Combe, often referred to as the quintessential Cotswold village, awaits your exploration. Its picturesque streets and medieval architecture exude an ageless allure. Allow yourself to be transported back in time as you meander through this living storybook village. Take a moment to savor tea in a local tearoom, soaking in the ambiance that surrounds you.

Day 4: Blenheim Palace - A Glimpse into Royalty

Today, you'll step into the opulent world of Blenheim Palace, a UNESCO World Heritage Site and the birthplace of the legendary Sir Winston Churchill. The palace's majestic architecture and meticulously landscaped gardens paint a vivid picture of centuries gone by. Wander through the grand halls that have borne witness to history, and traverse the parklands designed by Capability Brown, reveling in the grandeur that defines this magnificent estate.

Day 5: Stow-on-the-Wold and its Medieval Marvels

Stow-on-the-Wold, a market town steeped in history, invites you to discover its hidden gems. The imposing St. Edward's Church stands as a testament to medieval craftsmanship, its architecture an awe-inspiring sight. The Market Square, adorned with a mosaic of charming shops and eateries, creates the perfect backdrop for a leisurely afternoon. Every cobblestone whispers tales of times long past.

Day 6: Chipping Campden and Hidcote Manor Garden

Chipping Campden welcomes you with its High Street, adorned with honey-colored buildings that seem to radiate warmth. Here, you'll have the opportunity to explore Hidcote Manor Garden, a masterpiece of Arts and Crafts design. The intricacy of the garden's layout and the explosion of colors create an enchanting experience, showcasing the harmonious beauty that nature and human creativity can achieve together.

Day 7: Bourton-on-the-Water - The Venice of the Cotswolds

Known as the 'Venice of the Cotswolds', Bourton-on-the-Water beckons with its charming stone bridges that span the serene River Windrush. Take a leisurely stroll along the riverbanks, perhaps indulging in a riverside picnic, and explore the Cotswold Motoring Museum, a treasure trove of vintage automobiles and motoring memorabilia.

Day 8-14: Extended Exploration

For the remainder of your grand tour, the days are yours to savor at your own pace. You have the luxury of time to revisit favorite spots, uncover hidden gems, and explore the lesser-known corners of the Cotswolds. Consider taking a scenic walk along the Cotswold Way, which offers breathtaking views of the rolling countryside. Immerse yourself in the tranquil ambiance of the region, savoring moments of solitude and reflection.

Day 14: Farewell to the Cotswolds

As your two-week journey through the Cotswolds draws to a close, take a moment to reflect on the myriad experiences that have enriched your time here. Bid adieu to this enchanting region, knowing that the memories of its picturesque villages, historic landmarks, and breathtaking landscapes will remain etched in your heart forever.

This two-week grand tour is a celebration of the Cotswolds in all its splendor. It provides the space and time to delve deeper into the layers of culture and nature that define this region. Every day, every village, every landmark unravels a new story, ensuring that this journey will be a cherished memory for years to come.

11.3 Family-Friendly Adventure

Overview:

Embark on a week-long family-friendly adventure tailor-made to create treasured memories for all. This carefully crafted itinerary is designed with families in mind, offering an array of activities that cater to various ages and interests. From interactive exhibits at the Cotswold Motoring Museum to idyllic picnics by the riverside in Bourton-on-the-Water, there's something for everyone. Engage in hands-on pottery making and embark on scenic walks that promise both excitement and discovery. This adventure is your passport to forging lasting bonds and creating cherished moments with your loved ones.

Day 1: Arrival and Settling In

As you arrive in the Cotswolds, the excitement is palpable. Your family-friendly adventure begins with a warm welcome to your chosen base. Take the day to settle in, allowing everyone to get accustomed to the charming surroundings. Unwind and prepare for the days of exploration that lie ahead.

Day 2: Cotswold Motoring Museum - An Interactive Journey Through History

Today, the Cotswold Motoring Museum awaits, promising an interactive journey through the history of automobiles. From vintage cars to motoring memorabilia, there's something to captivate visitors of all ages. Watch as the little ones' eyes light up at the sight of these mechanical marvels, and let the fascinating exhibits transport you back in time.

Day 3: Bourton-on-the-Water - Riverside Picnics and Family Fun

Bourton-on-the-Water, known as the 'Venice of the Cotswolds', invites your family for a day of riverside enchantment. Stroll along the stone bridges that span the gentle River Windrush, and find the perfect spot for a picturesque family picnic. The kids can dip their toes in the water while you soak in the tranquil ambiance. Explore the village's quaint shops and perhaps indulge in some traditional Cotswold treats.

Day 4: Pottery Making - Unleash Your Creativity

Today is a day for hands-on creativity as you try your hand at pottery making. Engage in a fun and educational activity that promises to be a hit with both the young and the young at heart. Under the guidance of skilled artisans, each family member can create their own masterpiece, leaving with a tangible reminder of this special adventure.

Day 5: Family-Friendly Hikes - Discovering Nature's Wonders

Embark on a family-friendly hike along the scenic trails of the Cotswolds. Choose a route that suits the energy levels of your group, ensuring that everyone can enjoy the beauty of the countryside at their own pace. Along the way, keep an eye out for the diverse flora and fauna that call this region home. It's a day of exploration and discovery that promises to be both invigorating and educational.

Day 6: Further Adventures and Exploration

With the groundwork laid for your family's Cotswolds adventure, today is open for further exploration. Consider revisiting favorite spots or venturing into new corners of the region. The Cotswolds offer an abundance of activities, from charming village strolls to visits to local attractions. This day is yours to tailor to your family's unique interests and preferences.

Day 7: Culinary Delights and Farewell Celebrations

Immerse yourselves in the culinary delights of the Cotswolds. Sample local specialties and savor the flavors of the region at family-friendly eateries. As the day draws to a close, perhaps gather for a celebratory meal to toast to the memories you've created together.

Day 8: Departure and Reflections

As your family-friendly adventure in the Cotswolds comes to an end, take a moment to reflect on the experiences that have brought your family closer together. Bid farewell to this enchanting region, knowing that the memories of your time here will be cherished for years to come. This adventure has not only created moments to treasure but has also laid the foundation for future family explorations and bonding.

11.4 Solo Traveler's Journey

Duration: 10 Days

Overview:

This 10-day itinerary is tailored for the intrepid solo traveler, offering an enriching experience in the heart of the Cotswolds. It's an adventure crafted to celebrate independence, self-discovery, and the pure joy of solo exploration. Throughout your journey, you'll have the opportunity to join guided tours, providing an excellent chance to meet fellow enthusiasts. Yet, there will also be ample time for solitary walks along the famed Cotswold Way, and moments of quiet reflection in the region's charming villages. This itinerary is designed to embrace the freedom of solo travel and allow you to fully immerse yourself in the beauty and culture of this timeless English countryside.

Day 1: Arrival and Settling In

As you arrive in the Cotswolds, a sense of anticipation fills the air. Your solo adventure begins with a warm welcome to your chosen base. Take the day to settle in, allowing yourself to become familiar with the tranquil surroundings. Embrace the sense of freedom and look forward to the days of exploration that lie ahead.

Day 2: Guided Tour of Bibury and Castle Combe

Join a guided tour of two of the Cotswolds' most enchanting villages - Bibury and Castle Combe. This not only offers you a deeper insight into their history and significance but also provides an opportunity to meet fellow travelers who share your appreciation for the region's beauty. As you explore the timeless streets and soak in the atmosphere, you'll find that even in the company of others, there's a special kind of solace in solo travel.

Day 3: Stow-on-the-Wold - Market Town Majesty

Today, embark on a solitary journey to Stow-on-the-Wold, a market town that stands as a testament to centuries of history. Wander through the streets, absorbing the grandeur of St. Edward's Church and the vibrant energy of the Market Square. This is a day to revel in the quiet moments of reflection and to savor the beauty that surrounds you.

Day 4: Blenheim Palace - Solo Reflections in Grandeur

Visit the grandeur of Blenheim Palace, an architectural masterpiece set within captivating parklands. The vastness and beauty of the palace provide a perfect backdrop for solitary reflection. As you stroll through its halls and gardens, take in the rich history and revel in the sense of wonder that solo exploration can bring.

Day 5: Solo Walk Along the Cotswold Way

Today, set out on a solo walk along a section of the Cotswold Way, a trail that offers stunning vistas of the countryside. The tranquility of the path and the breathtaking scenery create an environment conducive to introspection and self-discovery. It's a day to revel in the freedom of the open road and to let the beauty of nature inspire your thoughts.

Day 6: Bourton-on-the-Water - Solitude by the Riverside

Bourton-on-the-Water, often referred to as the 'Venice of the Cotswolds', welcomes you for a day of serene solitude. As you stroll along the riverbanks and find a quiet spot for contemplation, you'll experience the unique charm of this village. This is a day to lose yourself in the beauty of the moment and to savor the peace that solo travel brings.

Day 7: Quiet Moments in Chipping Campden

Explore Chipping Campden, a village known for its stunning High Street and historic charm. Wander at your own pace, allowing the beauty of the architecture to captivate you. This day is yours to fill with moments of quiet reflection and to appreciate the simplicity and grace that the Cotswolds offer.

Day 8: Further Solo Adventures

With the foundation of your solo Cotswolds journey laid, today is open for further exploration. Consider revisiting favorite spots, venturing into new corners of the region, or simply allowing the day to unfold with spontaneity. The beauty of solo travel lies in the freedom to choose your own path.

Day 9: Culinary Delights and Farewell

Immerse yourself in the culinary delights of the Cotswolds. Sample local specialties and savor the flavors of the region at establishments that welcome solo diners. As the day comes to a close, perhaps gather your reflections over a final meal, celebrating the unique experiences that solo travel has brought to light.

Day 10: Departure and Reflections

As your solo adventure in the Cotswolds draws to a close, take a moment to reflect on the experiences that have enriched your time here. Depart knowing that the memories and insights gained from this journey will remain with you, a testament to the unique joys of solo exploration. This adventure not only celebrates independence but also leaves the door open for future solo escapades, each one promising new discoveries and self-discovery.

11.5 Romantic Getaways
Duration: 5 Days

Overview:

Embrace the allure of romance on a 5-day escape to the Cotswolds, a region known for its timeless beauty and intimate charm. This carefully curated itinerary is tailored for couples seeking a tranquil getaway, promising to kindle sparks and create cherished memories. Hand-in-hand, you'll wander through picturesque gardens, share intimate moments in cozy village inns, and indulge in candlelit dinners with breathtaking views. This journey is designed to be a tapestry of romantic experiences, set against the idyllic backdrop of the Cotswolds.

Day 1: Arrival and Romantic Stroll

As you arrive in the Cotswolds, a sense of romance permeates the air. Your romantic escape begins with a warm welcome to your chosen base. After settling in, set off on a leisurely stroll through the quaint streets, hand-in-hand with your beloved. Let the ambiance of this timeless region set the stage for the days of romance that lie ahead.

Day 2: Hidcote Manor Garden - A Love Story in Bloom

Begin your day with a visit to Hidcote Manor Garden, an enchanting masterpiece of Arts and Crafts design. Stroll together through the intricately designed garden, where each turn reveals a new facet of natural beauty. The intimacy of the setting provides the perfect backdrop for stolen glances and quiet moments of connection.

Day 3: Bourton-on-the-Water - Riverside Romance

Bourton-on-the-Water, known as the 'Venice of the Cotswolds', beckons for a day of riverside romance. Stroll along the stone bridges that span the serene River Windrush, hand in hand with your loved one. Find a quiet spot for a leisurely picnic, where you can savor the flavors of the region and each other's company. This is a day to let the beauty of the moment create lasting memories.

Day 4: Romantic Dinner with a View

As the sun sets, indulge in a candlelit dinner with a view. Choose from one of the region's picturesque eateries, where you can savor exquisite cuisine while gazing out at the breathtaking Cotswold landscape. The combination of fine dining and the natural beauty that surrounds you sets the stage for an evening of unparalleled romance.

Day 5: Farewell and Reflections

As your romantic escape draws to a close, take a moment to reflect on the moments of connection and intimacy that have enriched your time in the Cotswolds. Bid adieu to this enchanting region, knowing that the memories of your idyllic getaway will be cherished for years to come. This journey has not only kindled romance but has also set the foundation for future adventures and shared experiences that will continue to deepen your bond.

This 5-day romantic escape promises a tapestry of intimate moments against the backdrop of the Cotswolds' timeless beauty. From enchanting gardens to riverside strolls, every experience is designed to create cherished memories for couples seeking a tranquil getaway. It's a journey that celebrates love and connection, leaving you with a treasure trove of romantic moments to carry with you.

Note: Depending on your travel goals as stated in chapter one of this travel guide and the type of travel itinerary you would like to go for, you can still add some places you would like to visit which were not included in your choice travel itinerary, you can adjust any of them to suit your travel goals so as to a have an enjoyable and memorable trip.

CHAPTER TWELVE

COTSWOLDS PRACTICAL TIPS AND RESOURCES

12.1 Language Phrases

While English is the primary language spoken in the Cotswolds, it's always appreciated when visitors make an effort to use some basic local phrases. Here are a few helpful expressions:

Hello - "Good day!"

Thank you - "Thank 'ee" (informal) or "Thank you very much" (formal)

Please - "If you please"

Excuse me - "Beggin' your pardon"

Yes - "Aye" or "Yea"

No - "Nay"

Goodbye - "Cheerio" or "Ta-ta"

12.2 Sustainable Travel Practices

The Cotswolds, renowned for its breathtaking natural scenery, is a treasure trove of pristine landscapes. To safeguard this environment, it's imperative to adopt sustainable travel practices. Here are some valuable tips to consider:

Use Public Transportation: Embrace the convenience and eco-friendliness of public transit. Trains and buses are excellent options for traversing the Cotswolds, minimizing your carbon footprint in the process.

Explore on Foot or Bike: Immerse yourself in the beauty of the Cotswolds by taking advantage of the extensive network of walking and cycling trails. This not only offers a more intimate experience with the countryside but also significantly reduces environmental impact.

Support Local Businesses: Opt for accommodations, dining establishments, and shops that are proudly locally-owned. By doing so, you contribute directly to the region's economy, ensuring its long-term prosperity.

Reduce, Reuse, Recycle: Responsible waste management is paramount. Properly dispose of your waste in designated bins and consider adopting reusable practices. Carry a refillable water bottle and bring along reusable shopping bags to minimize single-use plastics.

Respect Wildlife and Nature: Preserve the delicate balance of ecosystems by treading lightly. Stay on designated paths to prevent soil erosion and avoid disturbing wildlife. Observing from a respectful distance allows you to appreciate the natural world without causing harm.

Incorporating these sustainable practices into your Cotswolds adventure not only enriches your experience but also leaves a positive mark on this extraordinary landscape. Together, we can ensure that future generations continue to revel in the unspoiled beauty of this remarkable region.

12.3 Health and Safety

Prioritizing your well-being is paramount during your visit to the Cotswolds. Here are essential tips to keep in mind:

Travel Insurance: Before embarking on your journey, ensure you have comprehensive travel insurance that covers medical emergencies. This safety net provides peace of mind, knowing you're protected in unforeseen circumstances.

Stay Hydrated and Sun-Safe: The Cotswolds' rolling hills and scenic trails beckon exploration, but it's crucial to stay hydrated, especially on warm days. Carry a refillable water bottle and drink regularly. Additionally, shield yourself from the sun's rays by wearing a wide-brimmed hat and applying sunscreen. This precautionary measure safeguards against sunburn and heat-related issues.

Watch Your Step: While the Cotswolds offer a plethora of enchanting footpaths, some areas may have uneven terrain. Exercise caution, especially when venturing into less developed areas. Sturdy footwear with good traction is recommended to prevent slips or falls.

Emergency Services: Familiarize yourself with the emergency services contact number: 999 (or 112). In case of any medical emergencies, quick access to professional assistance is crucial for your well-being.

Local Medical Facilities: Familiarize yourself with the location of the nearest medical facility or hospital. Having this knowledge ensures you can seek prompt medical attention if needed.

Insect Protection: In rural areas, especially during warmer months, insect repellent can be a valuable companion. It safeguards against bites from mosquitoes and ticks, offering an added layer of protection.

Traffic Safety: If you're exploring by road, remember that traffic may be different from what you're accustomed to. Keep to designated pedestrian areas and use crosswalks when available.

Personal Health Considerations: If you have specific health needs or require regular medication, ensure you have an ample supply for the duration of your stay. Additionally, carry any necessary documentation related to your health condition.

By adhering to these health and safety guidelines, you can fully immerse yourself in the beauty of the Cotswolds, confident that you're taking every precaution to ensure a safe and enjoyable experience.

CONCLUSION

Fond Farewells and Future Adventures

As the Cotswolds fade into the distance, remember that this chapter is but one verse in the epic ballad of your travels. The memories you've etched into these ancient stones and rolling hills will be your steadfast companions on the road ahead. Carry the Cotswolds within you, its beauty and history intertwined with your own story.

Whether you choose to revisit these cherished villages or set forth into uncharted territories, let every step be a dance of wonder and discovery. The world awaits, ready to reveal its secrets and unveil its marvels. The Cotswolds, with its open arms and timeless allure, will always be here to welcome you back, to pen new verses in your ever-evolving travel narrative.

As you embark on this new leg of your journey, may your experiences be as boundless as the horizon that stretches before you. Let the Cotswolds be your guiding star, illuminating the path to fresh and exciting destinations. Just as the golden hues of its cottages warmed your heart, may the memories of this enchanting region continue to kindle your spirit as you explore new corners of the world.

Until the day we reunite with the Cotswolds, may your adventures be imbued with the same magic that graced your time here. May each sunrise bring new revelations, and every sunset paint the sky with hues of wonder. Carry the Cotswolds' legacy of timeless beauty and warm-hearted hospitality with you, and let it infuse every step of your journey. Farewell for now, dear traveler, for the world beckons, eager to be discovered by you.

Made in United States
North Haven, CT
30 November 2023

44820299R00108